# How to Keep and Breed
# TROPICAL FISH

ISBN 0-87666-499-0

# How to Keep and Breed
# TROPICAL FISH

DR. C.W. EMMENS

**Title page photo:** A prize-winning planted aquarium by John LaPlante.

**Photo credits:** Courtesy of Artemia Reference Center, page 81 (top); Dr. Herbert R. Axelrod, pages 17 (top), 40 (top), 42 (bottom), 44 (bottom), 52 (bottom), 72 (top), 73, 89 (top), 108 (top), 109 (top), 121 (bottom); H. Azuma, page 117; K. Brauner, page 230; M. Chvojka, page 212 (top); Courtesy Danner Mfg., Inc., page 164 (bottom, left); S. Eden, page 49 (bottom); J. Elias, pages 33 (bottom), 207 (bottom); S. Frank, page 92 (top); Dr. R. J. Goldstein, pages 88 (top), 247 (bottom); Courtesy of Hagen Corp., pages 139 (bottom), 150, 172 (top); H. Hansen, page 44 (top); T. J. Horeman, page 36 (bottom); D. Howard, page 13 (bottom); J. Kassanyi, page 63 (bottom); Courtesy of Kordon, page 139 (top, right); Ken Lucas, Steinhart Aquarium, page 69 (bottom); G. Marcuse, page 39 (bottom); C.O. Masters, pages 80 (bottom), 81 (bottom); A. Noznov, pages 68 (top), 109 (bottom); A. van den Nieuwenhuizen, pages 36 (top), 121 (top); Courtesy of Odell Mfg. Co., page 13 (top); Courtesy of Mr. and Mrs. W. Paccagnella, page 128; Courtesy of Penn Plax Plastics, Inc., pages 139 (top, left), 164 (top), 196 (top); Dr. L. E. Perkins, pages 16 (bottom), 238 (top); H. J. Richter, pages 40 (bottom), 49 (top), 52 (top), 53, 56, 60, 61, 69 (top), 76 (bottom), 85, 92 (bottom), 93 (bottom), 100, 101, 104, 105, 125; J. Ronay, page 8; A. Roth, pages 48, 57 (bottom), 72 (bottom), 84, 112, 113, 124, 125 (top); Dr. H. Schneider, page 17 (bottom); Dr. G. Schubert, pages 231, 247 (top); Dr. C. D. Sculthorpe, page 16 (top); V. Serbin, pages 12, 107, 130, 164 (top, left); Courtesy of Dr. D. Terver, Nancy Aquarium, pages 33 (top), 68, 195; Dr. G. J. Timmerman, pages 42 (top), 63 (top); W. Tomey, pages 37, 80 (top); Courtesy of Vortex Innerspace Products, Inc., page 169 (bottom); G. Wolfsheimer, page 64 (bottom); R. Zukal, pages 22 (bottom), 23, 26, 27 (bottom), 57 (top), 88 (bottom), 93 (top), 96, 97, 121, 206, 207 (top), 212 (bottom), 238 (bottom), 239, 249.

Distributed in the UNITED STATES by T.F.H. Publications, Inc., 211 West Sylvania Avenue, Neptune City, NJ 07753; in CANADA by H & L Pet Supplies Inc., 27 Kingston Crescent, Kitchener, Ontario N2B 2T6; Rolf C. Hagen Ltd., 3225 Sartelon Street, Montreal 382 Quebec; in ENGLAND by T.F.H. (Great Britain) Ltd., 11 Ormside Way, Holmethorpe Industrial Estate, Redhill, Surrey RH1 2PX; in AUSTRALIA AND THE SOUTH PACIFIC by T.F.H. (Australia) Pty. Ltd., Box 149, Brookvale 2100 N.S.W., Australia; in NEW ZEALAND by Ross Haines & Son, Ltd., 18 Monmouth Street, Grey Lynn, Auckland 2 New Zealand; in SINGAPORE AND MALAYSIA by MPH Distributors Pte., 71-77 Stamford Road, Singapore 0617; in the PHILIPPINES by Bio-Research, 5 Lippay Street, San Lorenzo Village, Makati, Rizal; in SOUTH AFRICA by Multipet Pty. Ltd., 30 Turners Avenue, Durban 4001. Published by T.F.H. Publications Inc., Ltd., the British Crown Colony of Hong Kong.

# CONTENTS

Beginning hobbyists find artificial plants not only satisfactory in appearance but also sanitary and convenient. They require very little maintenance; regular rinsing in a commercial cleansing agent and water will be sufficient.

# CHAPTER ONE

## The Modern Aquarium

There are two main types of freshwater aquarium - those in which are collected together attractive and compatible fishes and plants regardless of the locality from which they come, and those in which an attempt is made to copy a natural piece of scenery, with rocks, plants and fishes which are normally found together. The latter type is increasingly seen in hobbyists' collections, but the majority of fish tanks will probably always be of the first type. In it, a purely artificial scene is built up to please the aquarist and not to copy nature, which can only be done in a superficial way in a small tank anyway. As long as they are properly looked after, the fishes don't mind, as far as we can tell!

In an aquarium, it is never possible to reproduce natural conditions, and the fishes live in an artificial environment which may include aeration, filtration, artificial light and heating, completely strange food and feeding regimes, water unlike their native water, and plants and other surroundings unlike those from which they or their ancestors came. Yet they may thrive, as do animals in captivity the world over. However, certain things must be done for them. Their surroundings must provide adequate shelter, they must not be bullied by other fishes, and their food must contain the proper nutrients. They must not be overcrowded or unduly disturbed, and of course they must be kept within tolerable temperature limits. Given these conditions, the fishes should grow and behave naturally, the best criterion of which is that they will reproduce, or at least be capable of reproduction.

Yet as with animals in a zoo, the fishes are unlikely to breed, or if they breed the young are unlikely to thrive, unless certain other factors are "right." These will often include factors quite irrelevant to the successful keeping of the fishes themselves, which are often far more tolerant of change than their germ cells or the fertilized egg. To breed, many fishes, particularly egg-laying fishes, may, therefore, demand a different set of conditions from those in which they may successfully be kept without breeding. Commonly they must be isolated from fishes other than a mate, the water must be of a certain quality, the temperature higher, and the surroundings different from those in a community tank. Even live-bearing fishes need a change in surroundings if many young are to survive. However, the conditions for successful breeding and rearing in a tank may not very closely resemble those in nature or resemble them at all. Indeed, some fishes have been found to have several alternative ways of reproducing, only one of which may resemble a natural one, if any of them do. Some of the killifishes are remarkable in this regard and may propagate with or without the drying of their eggs or may deposit their eggs differently according to circumstances.

## THE RECTANGULAR TANK

In later chapters we shall see clearly why the old-fashioned fish bowl is entirely unsuited to its purpose. It has been almost completely replaced for serious fish-keeping by the rectangular glass tank, either made wholly of glass or with a metal frame and glass sides and a bottom of glass, slate, or other rigid material. Except when used for spawning, for exhibition purposes, or as a hospital tank for the treatment of disease, the tank contains growing, rooted plants; these are set in a sand or gravel layer up to 5 cm or more thick. There may be decorative rocks, but the chief decoration is usually the plants themselves, which contribute more to the attractive appearance of a well set-up tank than do the fishes.

Such a tank is usually between 20 and 100 liters in capacity; a 60-liter tank measures 60x30x35 cm and is a favorite size. Smaller tanks than these cannot house many fish or allow proper development of the plants. Larger tanks are very attractive and give scope for beautiful planting arrangements and for fine growth of the fishes. Most fanciers therefore prefer a range of medium tanks rather than one or two very large ones, but it must be emphasized that fine fishes can be grown in large tanks.

In general, tropical fishes can be housed in smaller tanks than coldwater fishes. This is because they are usually smaller and are also better able to withstand a relative deficiency of oxygen in the water. Size for size, most tropical fishes can be crowded a good deal more than the common goldfish and very much more than fancy varieties of goldfish. A 60-liter tank might comfortably contain a dozen 7.5 cm rosy barbs, four or five 7.5 cm common goldfish at the most, and not more than a pair of orandas of the same size.

## THE BALANCED AQUARIUM

Animals (including fishes) consume solid food and excrete solid feces. They breathe oxygen and exhale carbon dioxide, and thus in total they tend to deplete their environment of oxygen and to foul it with carbon dioxide and excrement.

Plants also breathe oxygen, but in sufficiently bright light they manufacture sugars, etc., from carbon dioxide taken from their surroundings, whether air or water, and they release oxygen. This is done in the green leaf. They also absorb dissolved salts and use these together with carbon dioxide in building up complex organic compounds. Very few higher plants can utilize solid or very complex substances, and before animal excrement (forming part of the "mulm" in the fish tank) is available to them it must be broken down by fungi or bacteria and made soluble.

Thus plants, in adequate light, tend to restore oxygen to the environment and to remove the waste products of animals. In poor light or in darkness they deplete the water or air of oxygen just as animals do. It is only in the daytime, or under bright artificial light, that they perform the complementary function to animals.

From these facts grew the concept of a balanced aquarium, with the waste products of the fishes absorbed by the plants and the oxygen necessary for the fishes provided by the action of the plants in light. We shall see in later chapters how this idea must be modified in practice, but the basic principle is nevertheless sound, and a well-planted tank with adequate illumination will usually stay clear and sweet for months or years with little attention.

## AQUARIUM PLANTS

There are three main types of water plants of importance to aquarists—rooted plants, rootless plants, and floating surface plants.

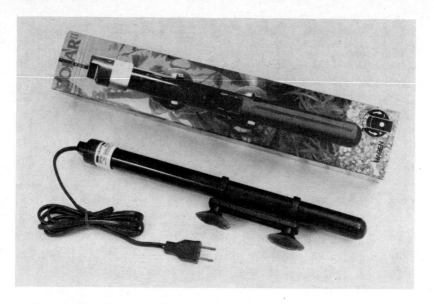

Get a good and sturdy heater that can withstand prolonged use. Take the water temperature regularly; extreme fluctuations can be fatal to some species of fish.

The members of the family can share the responsibilities of keeping the aquarium in good condition.

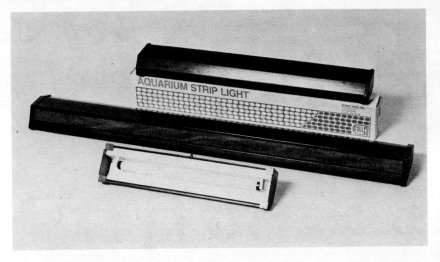

An aquarium lighting setup includes a permanent hood and a replaceable fluorescent tube. Lighting setups with tubular incandescent bulbs are also available.

If it is not possible for a planted aquarium to receive natural light, a special type of lamp that emits light rays needed by plants can be used.

*Rooted plants* are anchored in the sand at the bottom of the tank and their leaves grow toward the source of light. The grass-like varieties, *Vallisneria, Sagittaria,* and *Eleocharis,* exist in many types, from inch-high dwarfs to large plants with wide straps of leaves several feet long. They reproduce by runners, which bud off new plants, and these runners may lie along the surface of the sand or penetrate beneath it. They can also reproduce by surface flowers, but this method is of no practical importance to the aquarist.

Other rooted plants, such as *Echinodorus,* the Amazon sword plants, of which there are many varieties, reproduce much as do the foregoing, while others such as *Hygrophila, Myriophyllum,* and *Ambulia* will strike roots from almost any piece thrust into the sand. *Anacharis* or *Elodea,* also put out roots all over, and in nature the long growing stem is anchored by them as they penetrate the soil. All the foregoing plants are good oxygenators and absorbers of carbon dioxide and are fast growers—the two characteristics are probably quite highly correlated.

The cryptocorynes are beautiful, slower growing plants which can stand weaker lighting than most others and are really bog plants. They are not particularly useful as mulm and carbon dioxide users, but their splendid appearance makes them very popular, and, in addition, they last for years and gradually reproduce by offshoots from the base of the plant. *Ceratopteris* (water sprite or water fern) is a large fern-like plant which is very variable in form.

The *rootless plants* include *Ceratophyllum* (hornwort), which can be pushed into the sand and then looks much like *Ambulia* or *Myriophyllum,* and *Nitella,* both very useful for spawning as they form dense masses in mid-water. Both are good oxygenators and need good light to flourish.

*Floating plants* of importance are *Riccia, Salvinia,* and *Lemna* (duckweed). They are useful as top cover where the light is too strong, and the first two plants are also used in spawning tanks, as they form dense surface masses. *Salvinia* and *Lemna* are useless for oxygenation and carbon dioxide exchange as their leaves are above water, but they absorb waste matter from the tank.

*Cryptocoryne, Ambulia,* and *Echinodorus* are strictly warm-water plants, but the others mentioned above may be grown in either cold or warm tanks. *Vallisneria*, however, will not survive very cool conditions.

Various types of algae, either wanted or unwanted, occur in aquaria. They are practically absent from tanks which receive only artificial lighting, unless the light is very strong and prolonged. Filamentous green algae, chiefly the *Cladophora* types, are excellent food for many fishes and are also good oxygenators. Free-living green algae are important as food for fry, but they are unwanted in the usual tank, as they cloud the water. Blue-green algae (*Oscillatoria*, etc.) blanket other plants and may kill them. They also have an unpleasant smell and are ugly.

## MOLLUSKS

Aquarium snails consume algae and decaying vegetation. Very little damage to healthy plants is done by any commonly used species; most of them will not touch plants at all. The only obvious objection to some of the very large snails is that they may seriously foul the water when they die. A well-balanced tank can take the decease of smaller varieties in its stride, but the death of a large Japanese live-bearer may be too much for it.

The ramshorns (*Planorbis corneus*) are handsome snails, especially the red variety, which has a semi-transparent shell and a bright red body. The Australian red snail (*Bulinus australianus*) is of a similar color but whelk-like in shape. Other whelk-like snails are the *Limnaea* species, some of which are carnivorous and will help to clean up dead fish which may have become trapped and unnoticed at the rear of the tank. The winkle-like snails of the genera *Paludina* and *Viviparus* are live-bearing snails preferring cold to warm water, although *Viviparus* can tolerate tropical conditions fairly well. As remarked above, however, the popular Japanese live-bearer (*V. malleatus*) may grow too large for a small tank. The Malayan snail (*Melanoides tuberculata*) lives under the sand and makes a good job of cleaning it. This small brown-shelled conical snail may rarely be seen in daytime but emerges at night and may then be culled if necessary.

Many fishes attack snails and worry them to death. Some large fishes, such as cichlids, will eat all but the big ones whole. When they can survive, they are usually worthwhile additions to the

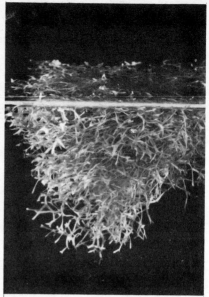

Left: *Salvinia* provides good top cover; it is especially useful in outdoor pools. **Right:** *Riccia* is a good spawning medium for bubblenest-building fishes like gouramis, paradise fish and Siamese fighting fish.

*Cabomba* will take root and grow well wherever it is planted, provided there are not too many fishes that can damage its fragile stems and leaves. Do not keep snails with this plant.

A small crayfish can add some color to a tank, but it can prey on small and sick fishes and can also ruin less sturdy aquarium plants.

The unsightly appearance of these guppies is caused by an infestation of parasitic larvae (glochidia) of a freshwater mussel. Fortunately, the infestation is of a temporary nature.

tank. They are good scavengers, and their eggs or young provide an occasional tidbit for the fishes. When too much prepared food has been used, snails may save the lives of the fishes by clearing it up before the water is fouled. Their capacity in this direction is not unlimited, however. In addition, all but some of the live-bearers are air-breathing and do not deplete the tank of any significant amount of oxygen. They crawl to the surface at intervals and take in air. They also absorb a little oxygen from the water, and if the tank is seriously depleted of oxygen they will remain at the surface and so act as indicators that all is not well.

Snails should be bred in fish-free tanks and fed on lettuce leaves or other dead or dying plant material. Well-fed and quickly grown specimens have clear, bright, and attractive shells.

Freshwater mussels rarely thrive in tropical tanks, and the larger varieties are a danger in any tank. It is not always easy to check that they are alive, and they may cause havoc in a tank if they die undetected. Also, some species, such as *Anodonta cygnea*, the swan mussel, free masses of larvae called glochidia which clamp onto fishes and live as parasites for some months before dropping off again. This method of dispersal does not commend itself to the aquarist, who would be foolish to risk keeping more than one mussel in a tank in any circumstances. However, as there are separate sexes, it is safe to keep a single individual. Even so, if it is a male, it may pour out swarms of spermatozoa and cloud the water. Finally, the larger varieties plow up the sand quite disastrously for carefully planned planting arrangements.

The main virtue of mussels is that they keep water clear, when not engaged in fouling it themselves. They live by filtering off microscopic food particles, living or dead, and they are useful for clearing up green water. On the whole, however, it is not advisable to have them as permanent aquarium inhabitants. Much the same situation holds for marine tanks. Various species of winkle and sea snails may be used, but the larger varieties are best avoided. Most are herbivorous and will not thrive unless provided with vegetable food, which is apt to be absent from marine tanks. Mussels may be used when small, but large mussels are dangerous for the reasons discussed above. Their function is often better performed by small sea squirts of various species, which each aquarist must discover in his own collecting ground or purchase from a supplier.

## OTHER TANK INHABITANTS

Except for the fishes and except when introduced as food, almost all other possible dwellers in the indoor freshwater aquarium are undesirable. Many prey upon fishes or the food of fishes, and some carry fish diseases. There are some insects and a few insect larvae which are harmless and could be kept with the fishes, but there seems little to commend them. Most large water beetles are carnivorous, and so are their larvae. Various worms and coelenterates are mostly pests and are dealt with in the appropriate chapter. Some corresponding inhabitants of marine tanks are, on the other hand, both harmless and beautiful. Some Crustacea are perfectly harmless, but as all but the largest are rapidly eaten by the fishes they do not remain on exhibition for very long.

## FISHES

Finally, we come to the fishes themselves. The main points of their anatomy and physiology are covered in the next chapter. Although this is not a book in which the various aquarium species will be described in detail, it seems a good place to outline the main families which are of importance to the aquarist and to mention some of their features. There are hundreds of families of fishes, and their exact definition varies with the authority, but those used in small aquaria number only a few dozen, and a mere eight or ten of them contain nearly all the common aquarium species.

All these families belong to the group Teleostei, or bony fishes. Those of most importance are:

*Characidae* - an enormous family (considered by some authorities as a group of many closely related families) of upwards of 2,000 species, nearly all small fishes, which make excellent aquarium inmates. They are characterized by having an adipose fin—a small knob of fat posterior to the dorsal fin - and hooks on the anal fin of the male. Not all species have these peculiarities, but most have at least one of them. They come from South America and Africa, with a representative from Texas. They are egg-layers and take no care of eggs or young once mating is completed.

Many characins have been bred in captivity for decades and are beginning to show the polymorphism characteristic of domestic animals. This means that generations of partial or even complete inbreeding have resulted in mutant strains becoming established, such as albinos, color varieties and long fins. They mostly prefer soft, acid water and may not survive, certainly not breed, unless given such conditions.

Outstanding examples of the family are the black tetra (*Gymnocorymbus ternetzi*), the red tetra (*Hyphessobrycon flammeus*), the glowlight tetra (*Hemigrammus erythrozonus*), the neon tetra (*Paracheirodon innesi*), the cardinal tetra (*Cheirodon axelrodi*), serpae tetras (*Hyphessobrycon serpae* and *H. rosaceus*), the head and tail light tetra or beacon fish (*Hemigrammus ocellifer*), and the pristella (*Pristella maxillaris*).

*Cyprinidae* - the carp family, which is found almost everywhere except South America and Australia (except as introductions). This family includes the goldfish, various attractive minnows, barbs, and the genus *Rasbora*. They are toothless, in contrast to the characins, and usually have one or more pairs of barbels hanging from the jaws. They are egg-layers and take no care of their young. The general run of barbs come from the Old World, mainly India and further east, the rasboras from Sumatra, Malaysia, and Borneo, with a few from India and Ceylon, while the danios have a similar range.

The barbs are old favorites—easy to breed, hardy, often with sex differences, usually with brighter males, which makes pairing off easy for the aquarist. Relatively few new species have been introduced recently and the existing species are, like the characins, beginning to show polymorphism. The rasboras are much harder to breed, although not hard to keep. Danios are ready breeders, hardy and splendid fishes which look best in schools.

Some outstanding examples of the family are the giant, zebra, and pearl danios (*Danio aequipinnatus*, *Brachydanio rerio*, and *B. albolineatus*), *Rasbora heteromorpha* (usually called just rasbora or, in Britain, the harlequin fish), various other *Rasbora* species, and the barbs, including the rosy barb (*Puntius conchonius*), the cherry barb (*Capoeta titteya*), the clown barb (*Barbodes everetti*), the black ruby barb (*Puntius nigrofasciatus*), the Sumatra barb (*C. tetrazona*), and the checker barb (*C. oligolepis*).

*Cyprinodontidae* - the oviparous toothcarps or killifishes—are also egg-layers, with teeth. They are sometimes called top minnows, from their habit of skimming near the surface of the water. They are found almost anywhere in the tropics, with examples from Europe and North America as well. They live in a variety of waters from brackish to soft and acid so that conditions for a particular species must be known if it is to thrive in captivity. These are fishes with a variety of methods of reproduction. The eggs of some species will survive drying up. Once dry, or nearly so, they can be kept, sometimes for months, and hatch on re-immersion. Thus, the Argentine pearlfish (*Cynolebias bellottii*) exists only as eggs for part of each year; these hatch out when the rains come and start a new generation of fish. These fishes never take care of their eggs or young, even when the adults survive.

Important members of the family are *Pachypanchax playfairii*, *Epiplatys chaperi* (Chaper's panchax), and a number of others grouped under the general name panchax: the blue gularis (*Aphyosemion sjoestedti*), the lyretail (*A. australe*), the Argentine pearl fish (*Cynolebias bellottii*), and various species of *Rivulus*, none of which have common names other than red, blue, or herringbone rivulus. The *Nothobranchius* species provide some spectacular fishes.

*Poeciliidae* - the viviparous toothcarps—having living young. While it seems reasonable to place them in a separate family, there is good evidence that live-bearers have arisen from cyprinodonts on a number of separate occasions and that they are really very closely related to them. This family includes the very popular guppies, platies, swordtails and mollies - easily bred old favorites.

The poeciliids come from Central and South America and the West Indies. They are scientifically interesting in many ways, having a placental system in some species which involves the heart membranes of the young and the ovary of the mother, from which blood-borne nourishment passes to the embryo. They also have internal fertilization, in that the male has a penis-like organ, the gonopodium, through which packets of sperm are placed into the female. These fishes will eat their young, but if plenty of cover is provided some will usually survive. The females produce several litters of young from one fertilization.

*Pachypanchax playfairii* is a well-known killifish that is kept by hobbyists around the world. It is colorful and easy to breed.

The presence of a "rivulus spot" in the female *Rivulus cylindraceus* easily distinguishes her from the spotless male.

The male *Nothobranchius rachovi,* like most other members of the genus, is strikingly colored and patterned, so differentiating the sexes is never a problem.

A pair of adult cherry barbs, *Capoeta titteya.* In many fish families the sexes are indistinguishable in the young stages, but during breeding the male becomes very colorful and the abdomen of the female enlarges considerably as eggs develop.

Fishes of particular interest in this family are the guppy (*Poecilia reticulata*), the platy or moon fish (*Xiphophorus maculatus*), the swordtail (*Xiphophorus helleri*), the mollies (*Poecilia latipinna* and others), and various hybrids between the platies and the swordtails, which have been so interbred that it is doubtful if any guaranteed pure stocks of either species are available except those recently caught from the wild. These fishes appear in a wide variety of color combinations. This group of fishes is more "cultivated" than perhaps any other but goldfish, and practically all available specimens are highly selected for color and often for finnage.

*Cichlidae* - largish, often pugnacious, "tough" fishes, which take care of their young in various interesting ways. Most of them guard the offspring throughout development, fanning the eggs and later herding the young into a compact swarm; some even starve throughout this period while keeping the young in their mouths. These fishes are found in Africa and in Central and South America; two species at least are found in India. In general, they are bad community fishes, particularly at breeding time, as they fight both with each other and with other species and often uproot plants. Only their interesting habits and the outstanding beauty of some have caused their continued popularity. There are a few species, such as the angels and *Aequidens portalegrensis*, which are reasonably peaceful, as are also the so-called dwarf varieties mentioned below.

The angelfish (*Pterophyllum scalare*) is probably the most important single aquarium fish, with the possible exception of the guppy. It has become available in various mutant forms, including jet black and veiltail types. Other important members of the family are the acaras (*Aequidens* species), the mouthbrooders (*Tilapia* species), the discus fishes (*Symphysodon discus* and *S. aequifasciatus*), the jewel fish (*Hemichromis bimaculatus*), the firemouth (*Cichlasoma meeki*) and the Jack Dempsey (*Cichlasoma octofasciatum*). The shy and attractive dwarfs, some still unidentified, belong to the genera *Nannacara* and *Apistogramma*, while the various *Pelvicachromis* species, particularly *P. pulcher*, represent beautiful African varieties.

Exploration of the African lake systems has revealed hundreds of new cichlid fishes, mostly inhabiting highly alkaline waters. Many are mouthbrooders, holding the eggs and young in the mouth for varying periods, or guarding them in the usual fashion. Popular among these new fishes are various *Pseudotropheus* species from Lake Malawi and various *Melanochromis* species from the same lake which although mostly aggressive, offer a series of beautifully colored fishes. *Pseudotropheus zebra* is remarkable in the great variety of colors and patterns it may exhibit - orange, red, blue, yellow, barred, or otherwise.

*Anabantidae* - the bubblenest builders. These fishes are found only in the tropical regions of the Old World, from Africa to the East Indies and China. Some authorities recognize several closely related families for these fishes. They possess an organ called the labyrinth, which is an extra air-breathing apparatus that makes its owner independent of dissolved oxygen in the water to a large extent and thus able to live in foul pools and streams. Air is gulped into the mouth at the surface and stored temporarily in the labyrinth. The habit of building bubblenests is a similar adaptation. The nest floats on the surface, and the eggs and young are brought into close contact with the air. The male fish guards the nest and renews the bubbles, and the family also contains a few mouthbrooders like the corresponding cichlids.

Important members of the family are the paradise fishes (*Macropodus* species), the Siamese fighting fish (*Betta splendens*), the various gouramis (*Colisa* species, *Trichogaster* species, and others), and the climbing perch (*Anabas testudineus*).

*Cobitidae* - the loaches are mostly bottom-living fishes from the Old World. Those of greatest aquarium interest are from Malaysia, Indonesia, and other parts of the East. They are scavengers and help to clear up uneaten food, but should be fed in addition to this. Favorite members are *Acanthophthalmus kuhlii*, the coolie loach, *Botia macracantha*, the clown loach, and *Botia hymenophysa*, the banded loach. None is easy to breed.

*Siluroids* - an old fashioned name for the catfishes, which are now divided into several families which will not be described separately. They are also bottom-feeders and scavengers, but some swim up into the water as well. There are some striking beauties in these families including *Synodontus angelicus*, the

The blue acara, *Aequidens pulcher* is a member of the large family Cichlidae. Cichlids are generally aggressive in temperament, particularly during the breeding phase.

The male croaking gourami, *Trichopsis vittatus,* constructs the bubblenest and will protect and care for the eggs. However, he will not hesitate to eat the fry later.

The polka-dot upside-down catfish, *Synodontis angelicus,* is quite efficient in scavenging and will consume uneaten food that, if left to decay, would quickly foul the water.

After repeated spawnings near the surface, this exhausted pair of loaches, *Acanthophthalmus myersi,* have returned to their normal position at the bottom of the tank.

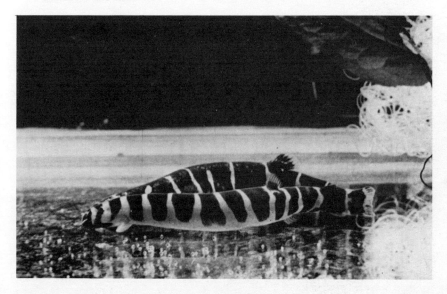

polka-dot upside-down catfish, many of the *Corydoras*, or armored catfishes, with hard rock-like bodies, and also some popular "uglies" such as *Loricaria parva*, the whip-tail catfish and *Hypostomus plecostomus*, the sucker catfish. Most of the species of aquarium interest come from South America.

## SPECIALIST TANKS

Although a tank may look beautiful, it may offend the purist because it contains rocks, animals, and plants coming from a variety of habitats without any sense of unity or pretense of looking like a pond or stream in a particular locality. Much the same is true of gardens, which may be purely decorative without reference to the natural location of each plant, or may be derived from a segment of bush, stream, or woodland.

As with many things, it is a matter of choice. The beginner always opts for a mixed bag of plants and fishes, choosing those which appeal to him without thought of from where they come. He may know enough to avoid mixing hard-water fishes with soft-water ones in the interest of their mutual welfare, but that is about as far as he is likely to go. Later, as is usual in public aquaria, he may choose to have tanks which reflect the plants and animals in a particular area, with water to match. An area such as a mangrove swamp, for instance, will have wood and not stone as a basic decoration and will have brackish water. A different kind of specialist might, however, keep killifishes irrespective of where they come from, or cichlids, being interested in types rather than localities. This may be quite reasonable and the aquarist in question may be interested in hybridizing his fishes, yet keeping stock in decorative tanks. The main point is to realize what you are doing and why you are doing it.

Examples of tanks copying specific environments are given below. As far as possible, the rocks, plants, and fishes are true to the areas concerned, with the proviso that in some cases the actual nature of the rock or gravel may have to be simulated rather than authentic, as in substituting granite for quartz, and that some of the plants may have to be as near as feasible to the natural ones—an African *Aponogeton* species might be substituted by one from Sri Lanka. Also, some plants now almost ubiquitous were originally confined to one area but have spread (or been spread) around the world—like *Elodea canadensis*, the Canadian water weed. In one case, the African lakes, the author has not been able to be sure which plants are found there and has made a guess from looking at underwater pictures taken at the site. A lot has been written about the fishes, little about the plants. At least the suggested species *look* right.

Here, then, are some suggested "aquascapes":

**Amazon Rivers:**

Roots, driftwood and darkish rock with coarse gravel form a suitable background in this type of aquarium, with a wealth of rooted and floating plants. Rooted plants should include the famous Amazon swords, of which there are many species ranging from giants to dwarfs. *Cabomba, Hygrophila, Sagittaria, Eleocharis, Salvinia, Azolla* and *Riccia* are other suitable plants. The varieties of appropriate fishes are vast. Any of the South American tetras, catfishes, pencilfishes, angels and discus are suitable, but most of them look best in schools with few species per tank. There are various types of water, from clear to cloudy and white to deep brown (the "black" water imitated in tanks by treatment with peat moss). However, all are soft, and clear white water of pH 4.5 to 6.5 at 20° to 30 °C is appropriate. Hardness should not exceed about 50 ppm, and for breeding, species such as neons require very soft water, less than about 15 ppm.

**Central American Hardwaters:**

For the keeping of most live-bearing fishes (the Poeciliidae) a tank with quite hard but not necessarily very alkaline water is needed. Up to 500 ppm hardness and pH around neutral is fine for guppies, for instance, although as we pass to swordtails, platies and further still to mollies an increasing pH and salinity are best. Mollies can stand full-strength sea water—so too can guppies, if gradually acclimatized to it.

As a planted tank is best for live-bearers, and plants cannot in general stand brackish water, the livebearer tank is nicest at about 300 to 400 ppm (15-20 German degrees of hardness) and mildly alkaline, say pH 7.5, so that the fishes will breed and thrive. Use root—driftwood—rock—gravel scenarios, with *Sagittaria, Cabomba, Ceratophyllum,* or *Myriophyllum,* with perhaps some hardy floating plants to help shelter the young. Temperatures can vary from 21° to 27°C.

## Malayan Streams:

These streams tend to have a rocky and pebbly base, with stones of various sizes and perhaps some roots, copied in the tank by driftwood. The water is very clear, soft and acid, pH 5.0 to 6.0, and at a temperature of 24° to 27°C or even higher. However, the fishes are quite happy at the lower part of the range. There is a wide choice of plants suitable to the locality, in which are found *Cryptocoryne* species, *Aponogeton*, *Hygrophila* and *Fontinalis*. Various loaches such as *Botia macracantha* and *B. hymenophysa*, labeos, barbs and rasboras are native to the area— just check before purchasing that the species you have in mind is suitable.

## African Lakes:

Recent concentration of ichthyologists and others on the eastern African lakes has provided dozens of new species of fishes from isolated areas in which they alone occur—particularly cichlids. Many of the lakes are large and deep, resembling inland seas, and it is only around their shores that vegetation (if any) and fishes are found. The lakes vary enormously in hardness and salinity and in the nature of their shores. It is thus necessary to decide on a type of locality to imitate.

Since the cichlid species are of most interest and many do not tolerate dense planting, it would be sensible to copy a rocky area with perhaps a sandy base and just a few plants. *Vallisneria* and *Cabomba* appear to grow in such localities, with fairly hard water at a pH of 7.7 to 8.6, important for the welfare of the fishes. Attractive species are *Melanochromis vermivorus*, *Pseudotropheus zebra*, and various *Haplochromis* species, which thrive at a temperature of 24° to 28°C.

## Brackish Water:

This aquascape is difficult to make very attractive as higher plants do not thrive in really brackish water. An imitation of a mangrove swamp would show tree roots (easily imitated with driftwood and safer than the real article) with perhaps a sparse growth of sedges, *Marsilea* or *Elodea* if the salinity were kept low. This is an instance where the fishes would form a primary attraction. They should include *Scatophagus argus*, especially the red (*rubrifrons*) variety, *Monodactylus argenteus*, *Periophthalmus* (the mud-skipper) and *Pseudomugil signifer* (the blue-eye). These fishes are happy at alkaline pH 7.5 to 8.5, in hard water, which need not in fact be very salty, and at temperatures of 21° to 27°C.

## BIOLOGICAL CYCLES

### The Nitrogen Cycle

Of several cycles taking place in natural waters and in the aquarium, the nitrogen cycle is the most important for the aquarist. It concerns the breakdown and eventual fate of products of decomposition, from uneaten food to feces and decaying plants, all of which contain organic nitrogen—compounds of varying complexity containing nitrogen, but eventually breaking down to simple compounds. Most of this breakdown is the work of bacteria which convert the waste products to ammonia, which exists in water in part as ammonium hydroxide ("liquid ammonia"), in part as ammonium and hydroxyl ions, and in part as dissolved ammonia gas:

$$NH_4OH \rightleftharpoons NH_4^+ + OH^- \rightleftharpoons NH_3 + H_2O$$

| ammonium hydroxide | ammonium and hydroxyl ions | dissolved ammonia gas |

The higher the pH, the more the equilibrium point is pushed towards the right hand side of the equation and the more free ammonia (dissolved ammonia gas) there is. Ammonia is a prime culprit in fish deaths and is more toxic than ammonium ions or ammonium hydroxide. It is not tolerated by fishes beyond a small fraction of a part per million. It is therefore essential to get rid of the ammonia, and this is done for us by further bacteria, which convert ammonia to nitrous acid derivatives.

Unfortunately, nitrous acid and its salts, the nitrites, are fairly poisonous at least to some fishes, so we are not much better off at that stage. Other bacteria luckily bring about a further conversion of nitrites to nitrates, which are no longer very toxic and can also be readily utilized by plants. This is the nitrification stage of the nitrogen cycle, which then continues into a build-up of

31

nitrogenous plant material which takes us back to one of the starting points of the cycle. Some plants can absorb ammonia as well, and some bacteria also carry the process further to produce free nitrogen gas, also harmless, but the main route of conversion is as described.

Kits are available for the measurement of ammonia, nitrites, and nitrates. The most valuable measurement in an established tank would be of the nitrite level. Once ammonia levels have reached a certain point, bacteria will become established, especially in a tank with an undergravel filter, which will rapidly convert ammonia to nitrites, which are more likely to accumulate and cause trouble than is dissolved ammonia gas. If any detectable level of nitrites exists, steps must be taken to correct the situation—water changes, less feeding, fewer fishes, and a general clean-up all help, as does better illumination for the plants, if felt to be needed, to increase their demand for nitrogenous materials. Nitrates only matter if over about 40 ppm, which is easily detected with a standard kit.

In a newly set-up aquarium, without an established population of bacteria to keep things in equilibrium—as long as maintenance is adequate—a phenomenon known as the new tank syndrome is liable to occur. Since ammonia is the first toxic product of waste material breakdown, and suitable bacteria for its conversion to nitrites may not yet be established, it is liable to build up to enormous levels relative to its toxicity, which is around 0.1 ppm. These may reach 5.0 to 10.0 ppm, with disastrous results. The same may occur with nitrites, because the bacterial population for their breakdown has also to be established, and as with ammonia, is not stimulated until the material on which it thrives has accumulated. So an ammonia peak will usually be followed by a nitrite peak, only later to die down with a steady production of nitrates and very low levels of the first two substances. In a salt water tank this regularly occurs, because few or no plants are available to deal with early production of ammonia or nitrites until algae may become established. In a freshwater tank, depending on circumstances, the phenomenon may be considerably modified, but few studies are available for our information. The presence of living, growing plants and the lower pH typical of the freshwater tank *may* save the day, but it may not, and

**Right:** Water sprite, *Ceratopteris thalictroides,* is a pleasing light green in color. It grows fast and can be cultivated as a floating plant at the top or as a rooting plant at the bottom of the tank. **Below:** *Vallisneria,* one of the most popular aquarium plants, enhances any tank and is especially attractive as a background plant. Different *Vallisneria* species develop leaves of various widths and forms: straight and flat, slightly twisted, and spirally twisted or coiled.

weakened fishes are very likely to break out with disease at this early stage.

## Other Cycles

A carbon dioxide cycle occurs to a limited extent in a planted tank, with plants in adequate light converting carbon dioxide to sugars and freeing oxygen into the water. The oxygen gas can be seen rising from the plant leaves as a string of bubbles in bright sunlight. However, as the plants are a detriment in poor light or in the dark, the cycle is irregular and of no permanent benefit. The water surface interchange of oxygen and carbon dioxide is far more important.

A phosphorus cycle also occurs, and may be stimulated if phosphate buffers are used. If over-used, and perhaps in combination with excess production of nitrates, algal "blooms" may occur in the aquarium and give rise to green water, which is essentially healthy but hides the fish and is not welcomed by the aquarist. It is dangerous to try to cure green water by cutting down the light drastically, as this may cause death of the algae and sudden, severe pollution. Similar excesses of nutrients in the water may also cause gray or white cloudy water due to bacteria, and usually occur in the absence of strong illumination. Both types of cloudiness need careful handling as described later.

# CHAPTER TWO

## The Anatomy and Physiology of Fishes

Fishes are cold-blooded vertebrates. This means that they remain at approximately the same temperature as the water surrounding them, in contrast to the whales, mammals which like ourselves maintain a much higher temperature. Aquarium fishes share with mammals, however, the possession of a backbone, or vertebral column, and are built on the same fundamental plan, having the same basic system of bones and organs as we do.

Fishes breathe oxygen, but it is usually absorbed only from solution in water by the *gills*, which are leaf-like organs, normally four on each side of the neck in a pouch covered by the *operculum*, or bony gill cover. The gills are richly supplied with blood vessels, and water is swallowed from the mouth and forced over the gills, leaving by a slit between the operculum and the body. The rate of fishes' respiratory movements is partly determined by the need for oxygen and its concentration in the surrounding water.

### BODY

The fish body is composed mainly of a large lateral muscle on each side of the backbone, divided by sheets of connective tissue into segments corresponding to the vertebrae, which give rise to the typical flaking of the cooked fish. This is the main organ for swimming. The internal organs often occupy a very small volume toward the front, so that much of the apparent trunk of the fish is really its tail (as distinct from the *tail fin*). This is indicated by the forward position of the beginning of the anal fin, which marks the end of the digestive tract. Fishes possess the usual organs familiar to students of human anatomy, with the exception of lungs and chest cavity; they have a stomach, intestines, a liver, a spleen, kidneys, and so forth.

Amazon sword
plants, genus
*Echinodorus,* make
good decorations in
community tanks,
and many fish
species spawn on
the sturdy leaves.
Amazon sword plants
are perennials and
do not undergo
hibernation in winter.

The *Hygrophila*
species available
commercially thrive
well under normal
aquarium conditions;
low temperatures do
not harm them but
can limit their
growth.

Under good illumination, *Elodea* is a prolific plant; it can grow in any type of water, including hard water which it softens by absorbing the limy salts.

*Myriophyllum,* commonly called milfoil, has fine leaves arranged in whorls. Like *Cabomba,* it is a good spawning and refuge plant.

*Skin and Scales.* The skin may be naked, or it may be covered by scales or by bony plates which in turn have an outer layer over them. The scales may be opaque or transparent; if they are transparent, the appearance and color of the fish may be due to skin pigments, not to scale color or formation, as in the calico goldfish. Bony plates may be seen in *Corydoras,* South American armored catfishes.

## FINS

There are two paired and (in all but some fancy goldfish and a few other fishes) three unpaired fins. The paired *pectoral* and *pelvic* (*ventral*) fins correspond, respectively, to the arms and legs of human beings and connect with bony girdles in the body which correspond to our own pectoral and pelvic girdles. The unpaired fins are the *dorsal*, the *anal*, and the *tail* or *caudal* fins. These fins are supported by rays, sometimes bony and sometimes segmented. In some families the dorsal fin is split entirely into two parts, the forepart with hard spines and the hindpart with soft rays. In the characins and some others, there is a small *adipose* fin, composed of fatty material with no fin rays.

## PECULIARITIES OF FISH ANATOMY

*Air Bladder.* Many fishes possess a characteristic organ, the air bladder. This is a long bag filled with gas and lying in the body cavity. It may be entirely closed, or it may communicate with the alimentary tract by means of a duct or tube. Sometimes it is divided into two rather distinct parts which communicate with each other. The air bladder controls the specific gravity of the fish, as the diving tanks of a submarine govern its buoyancy. In fishes with divided bladders, the center of gravity can be altered too. It actually corresponds to the lungs of higher vertebrates, and this fact is foreshadowed in the so-called lung fishes, which take air into their air bladders and breathe as we do.

*Labyrinth.* In the Anabantidae and other families, as mentioned in the preceding chapter, an entirely different organ, the labyrinth, is also used as an auxiliary air-breathing apparatus. This organ is situated near the gills, and air is passed through or

38

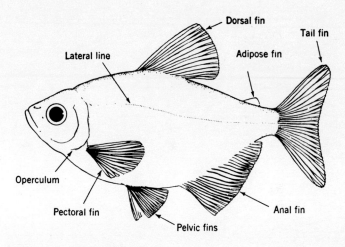

Finnage of a typical fish.

The celestial, a fancy breed of goldfish, lacks a dorsal fin. As a consequence, it can not swim as fast as a "wild type" goldfish with normal finnage.

Some genera of catfishes, *Clarias* as an example, have naked skin. For protection, the skin secretes much mucus, especially in species that leave the water to migrate over land.

*Corydoras aeneus,* representative of the South American armored catfishes, is bred commercially for fish hobbyists. The albino mutation of this species is very popular in the hobby.

Some of the fancy breeds of goldfish have atypical finnage; as seen here, the caudal and anal fins are split and all the fins are much longer than in the "wild type" goldfish.

This fish is not in distress or about to die. It is normal for the upside-down catfish, *Synodontis nigriventris,* to swim in such a position.

The outward manifestation of alternate muscle action is most evident in the swimming movement of an eel-like fish. It is quite possible that your local pet shop has white-spotted eels, *Mastacembelus armatus,* imported from the Far East.

into it and out through the mouth or gill slits.

*Lateral Line.* Careful examination of the majority of fishes will reveal a line running from the head along the side of the body. This is a series of tubes filled with a gummy secretion and with stiff bristles at the base. Its function is to detect vibrations of low frequency. The *ear* is a specialized part of the lateral line system.

*Nostrils.* It may seem odd that fishes have nostrils, but they do —in fact, they often have four of them. They are organs of smell and do not perform any function in breathing, since they do not open into the mouth.

## SWIMMING AND BALANCING

Most fishes swim by body movements, not fin movements. The fins are mainly balancers, with the exception of the tail fin, which often acts as a final thrusting member, propelling the fish through the water. In normal, medium-paced to fast swimming, the action is initiated at the head end of the fish, and waves pass down the body, culminating in a flick of the tail. The dorsal and anal fins prevent the fish from turning over in the water; the paired fins also perform braking and turning functions. In slow swimming and in static balancing in the water, the pectoral fins are used. These fins are usually colorless, so that when the fish is still in the water, their gentle movement is unnoticed. Indeed, in a fish like the Siamese fighting fish they have to be looked for quite carefully, in contrast to the bright colors of the rest of the finnage.

Some fishes, particularly some of the reef fishes and the sticklebacks, normally swim with the pectoral fins rather than the body, but this is an unusual habit.

The balance of fishes is controlled by three main factors.

1): *The inner ear* contains (as does ours) a system of sensitive sacs containing bones, called *otoliths*, which are balancing organs. The movement of the bones in the sacs tells the brain of the fish about its orientation and movements.

2): *The muscles* themselves convey messages of position and movement, and it is possible that the lateral line also does so. In a fish, it is likely that only active movements bring forth the inner ear and muscular perceptions. It has also recently been discovered that many fishes are equipped with a kind of radar

The mudskippers, *Periophthalmus,* need a terrarium-like setup with a dry place where they can climb occasionally. Note the dorsal placement of the eyes, an adaptation for aerial vision.

This fish has a well developed lateral line extending from the back part of the head to the base of the tail. Not all fishes have lateral lines, and, when present, they are very variable.

Having a labyrinth organ as well as gills permits the paradise fish, *Macropodus opercularis*, to utilize atmospheric air. Aeration is not strictly needed for keeping and breeding labyrinth fishes in tanks.

device, the muscles acting as broadcasters of electrical impulses which are reflected from surrounding objects. The main receptor organ is thought to be the lateral line.

3): *The eyes* are very important in most fishes, not merely for normal visual perception, but because the fish so adjusts itself, if possible, that the two eyes receive equal amounts of light. This is the same reaction that causes insects to fly into a light. In the aquarium, its effects are seen if the light entering the tank is not from overhead, when the fishes may be observed swimming along at an angle, sometimes a very odd sight. Continued slanting illumination is said to cause disorders in the fishes subjected to it.

## METABOLIC RATE AND OXYGEN NEED

The rate at which an animal uses up energy, produces heat and waste products, and consumes oxygen is called the metabolic rate. An understanding of the factors which modify it is of primary importance to the aquarist.

Since fishes are cold-blooded, they differ fundamentally from ourselves in that they have an increased metabolic rate as the temperature rises, and they are hungriest when warm. We consume a great deal of energy, which we get from our food, in maintaining our body temperature constant and normally well above that of our surroundings. A fish doesn't do this but merely obeys a basic chemical law which causes body processes to go faster the higher the body temperature. Thus a fish turns energy over at a much greater rate in warm water than in cold water.

Another factor influencing the metabolic rate is activity. A resting fish consumes less energy than an active fish. The higher the temperature, the more energetic a fish tends to be, so that an elevated temperature acts doubly in causing greater energy consumption in most species—the fish is using more energy not only because it is warmer but also because it has to swim more to catch and to consume and digest more food. This action has an upper limit, however, probably determined by the lowered solubility of oxygen in warmer waters. Thus, at about 27 °C, the average fish reaches its maximum oxygen consumption and maximum appetite.

46

A further factor influencing metabolism is age. Young fishes are growing relatively faster than older fishes, and also they use up oxygen and foodstuffs faster per unit of body weight. There are no exact recorded measurements for fishes, but if they are anything like birds and mammals in this respect the difference is one of several hundred percent—i.e., a gram of adult barb needs only a fraction of the oxygen per minute that a gram of young barb needs.

A final important factor, especially in live-bearers, is sex and pregnancy. Gravid female live-bearers need a good deal more oxygen than even younger fishes or males and will suffocate first in an overcrowded tank containing adults and young. This is because they are breathing for their young as well as for themselves.

## GROWTH, AGE, AND SIZE

In common with most living things, fishes grow most rapidly when they are young and gradually slacken off as they become older. Although there is an approximate maximum or fully grown size in most species, this maximum is really only the top of the growth curve, which does not flatten out entirely under favorable conditions, with plenty of food, oxygen, and room.

A starved or semi-starved growing mammal is likely to die and will certainly be stunted in growth. However, if it survives at all, it will not be *much* smaller than normal, although it will be thinner and wretched looking. A semi-starved fish may die, but if it lives it will grow very little or even not at all, and it may reach breeding age at a tenth of the normal weight. There are often tremendous differences among members of the same batch of fry growing under apparently identical conditions in the same tank. Some become so much larger than others that they can eat them, and so get larger still. This difference is usually seen when the baby fishes are underfed, so that the lucky ones happen to swallow most of the available food in the early stages or are hatched before the others and are then progressively better able to grab whatever comes, at the expense of their smaller brethren. When there is plenty of suitable food, much smaller differences are normally seen, and an even batch may frequently result in wildtype fishes such as barbs or characins. Fancy fishes, such as

The common Siamese fighting fish, *Betta splendens,* is well known and very popular all over the world for the bubblenesting habits of the very colorful males, which are also aggressive and are usually kept in isolation most of the time.

**Opposite page:** *Betta pugnax* (top) and *Betta macrostoma,* (bottom) unlike the common Siamese fighting fish, are mouthbrooders and not bubblenesters. Unfortunately, they do not breed well in captivity and are seldom available in pet shops.

some of the goldfishes, usually throw a fair proportion of runts even under good conditions, which would indicate a genetic rather than a nutritional cause.

Thus fishes of the same species may differ enormously in size at the same age, depending on the food and possibly the room available to them in their earlier stages. The exact extent to which swimming space really matters has not been determined, but it is suspected that, as long as adequate food and air are available, swimming space makes little difference and the apparent effects of crowding are usually due to insufficient food and air.

Starved fishes may catch up to the normal if given the chance, and it is not clear whether they can be permanently stunted within, say, a year or so of hatching. If kept on short rations for a longer period, the average aquarium fish is said to be permanently affected, but there seem to be no records substantiating this claim. The usual effect of aquarium life in itself is to stunt in comparison with the size found in the wild, with one or two very curious exceptions, such as *Copeina guttata*, which grows to 10 cm in the aquarium but has never been caught in nature longer than 7.5 cm. It has been found, however, that in very large tanks with everything as nearly perfect as possible, including much live food, fishes grow as large as in the wild. The limiting factors are probably oxygen and carbon dioxide exchange and adequate food, as noted above.

## SALT TOLERANCE AND EXCRETION

The kidneys and the gills are the most important of all the organs which regulate the composition of the blood in fishes. For life to continue, this must be kept remarkably constant, and small variations may lead to severe illness or death. Thus, oxygen, carbon dioxide, and some salts are exchanged in the gills, sometimes through the skin, and waste products such as uric acid or urea and excess salts, acids, or alkalis are passed out in the urine by the kidneys.

Fishes have to do one of two things. If the water in which they are swimming is saltier than their own blood, as in marine fishes, they must work continually to prevent themselves from being dehydrated and "pickled." This they do by excreting a lot of salt and comparatively little water. They swallow water and the salts it contains, and they pass a fairly dilute urine, most of the salt being excreted by special cells in the gills. If the water is fresh, they must work to prevent themselves from blowing up with water, for their saltier blood and tissues will normally tend to "clog up" with absorbed water. So in this case the fishes produce a copious stream of very dilute urine and, by means of other special gill cells, actively absorb such salt as is present in the surrounding water.

Some fishes can do *either* of these and can live in salt or fresh water, especially if not too suddenly plunged from one to the other. Others cannot tolerate such a change and can live only in one type of water, with a tolerance to minor variations which differs from species to species. The presence of calcium has been found to influence this ability, and marine fishes can sometimes stand transfer to brackish or practically fresh water as long as it is hard, i.e., calcium-containing. Thus, *Scatophagus argus*, a marine species often kept in freshwater aquaria, may be plunged directly into hard fresh water with little or no obvious discomfort, but in soft fresh water it dies, either rapidly or after a period of decline. Other species such as eels or salmon are indifferent even to calcium content.

At the other extreme are the pelagic marine fishes like herring, which are extremely sensitive to changes in salinity and cannot stand appreciable dilution of the sea water in which they live. However, most fishes are fairly tolerant of small variations. Most freshwater fishes can take up to about quarter-strength marine water, i.e., approaching the salinity of their own blood, whereas most seawater fishes can live comfortably in two-thirds-strength marine water, but not much less. In terms of specific gravity, with fresh water at 1.000 and sea water at 1.025 to 1.030, the majority of fresh-water species can stand salt up to a reading of about 1.0075, and the majority of marine species can stand dilution down to about 1.017. In percentages, full-strength sea water contains about 3.7% of dissolved solids, most of which is sodium chloride (common salt). A salt solution of about 37 grams per liter is equivalent in saltiness to sea water. Freshwater species may thus be expected to stand up to about 9 gm per liter, and some, such as guppies and mollies, can take more and be gradually acclimatized to sea water itself.

The spotted scat, *Scatophagus argus,* lives in the ocean and in brackish waters and should have a considerable salt content in its tank water.

The red-spotted copeina, *Copeina guttata,* is an exception to the rule that aquaria stunt fishes: it grows larger in captivity than in the wild. A good jumper, its tank should always be covered.

*Lamprologus brichardi* is an African import that is easy to breed. It is a small species reaching a maximum length of 9 cm in its natural habitat, Lake Tanganyika.

53

# TEMPERATURE TOLERANCE AND ADAPTABILITY

In general, fishes are adapted to the temperature variations of their natural surroundings and not much more. If a fish comes from a seasonally variable environment, in which it may stew in summer or freeze in winter, then, like the common carp, it can stand these extremes, but it cannot usually stand a *sudden* change from one to the other. If it comes from the rock pools of the seashore, like the goby, it may stew in an exposed small pool and then be flushed out by an incoming tide at a temperature 10° to 15°C below that of the pool. The goby can stand these extremes.

If, like the majority of marine fishes, the fish comes from a very constant environment in which it can move about so that even the slow changes in temperature can be avoided, it is likely to be very touchy about the temperature of its surroundings and therefore inadaptable.

The freshwater aquarium fishes tend to come from fairly still waters which may undergo fairly wide changes in temperature but which do not change suddenly. When these waters are tropical, their temperature does not drop below 18° to 20°C, but it may rise to over 38°C, and therefore tropical fishes can stand this kind of range. In the aquarium they tend to be less happy at the extremes of their natural tolerance than in the wild, and it is usual to try to keep the temperature within a range of say 21° to 27°C, with as short a period as possible beyond these limits, particularly downward.

The *sudden* exposure to a change in temperature of more than 1° to 2°C *downward* is likely to cause shock, followed by disease. For complete safety, it is best to avoid rapid change of more than 1°C or a slower change at a rate of more than about 3°C per hour covering a total change of 3°C downward and 8°C upward. A greater change than these may result in damage to most species, unless several days are taken up in achieving it. It has been found, however, that fishes arriving from a distance really chilled do better if they are placed immediately in water at 21° to 27°C than if time is wasted in raising the temperature slowly. The usual symptoms of chill are a very characteristic slow, weaving motion like slow-motion swimming without getting anywhere, often called "shimmies," and the development of a disease called

| FAMILY | GENUS OR SPECIES | NORMAL RANGE |
|---|---|---|
| Characidae | Most species | 20°-27°C |
| | *Copeina guttata* | 15°-27°C |
| | *Hemigrammus caudovittatus* (tet from Buenos Aires) | 15°-27°C |
| | *Ctenobrycon spilurus* | 15°-27°C |
| | *Aphyocharax anisitsi* (bloodfin) | 15°-27°C |
| | *Astyanax* | 18°-27°C |
| | *Carnegiella marthae* (hatchet fish) | 18°-27°C |
| | | |
| Cyprinidae | Most cold-water fishes | 2°-22°C |
| | Most goldfish varieties | 2°-27°C |
| | *Danio, Rasbora* | 20°-27°C |
| | *Brachydanio rerio* (zebra fish) | 15°-38°C |
| | Barbs | 18°-27°C |
| | *Barbodes everetti* (clown barb) | 20°-27°C |
| | *Puntius conchonius* (rosy barb) | 15°-27°C |
| | *P. vittatus* | 15°-27°C |
| | *Capoeta semifasciolatus* (half-banded barb) | 15°-27°C |
| | *Tanichthys albonubes* (white cloud mountain fish) | 5°-30°C |
| "Siluridae" | Most catfishes | 20°-27°C |
| | *Corydoras* | 15°-27°C |
| Cyprinodontidae | Most species | 20°-27°C |
| | *Oryzias latipes* | 5°-27°C |
| | *Aphanius* | 15°-32°C |
| | *Fundulus chrysotus* | 15°-27°C |
| Poeciliidae | Most species | 18°-27°C |
| | *Xiphophorus variatus* (platy variatus) | 10°-27°C |
| | *Gambusia affinis* | 10°-27°C |
| | *Heterandria formosa* | 10°-27°C |
| | *Phalloceros caudomaculatus* | 10°-27°C |
| | *Poecilia* (mollies) | 15°-27°C |
| | *Poecilia reticulatus* (guppy) | 15°-27°C |
| | *Xiphophorus maculatus* (platy) | 18°-32°C |
| | *Xiphophorus helleri* (swordtail) | 20°-32°C |
| Anabantidae | Most species | 20°-32°C |
| | *Macropodus opercularis* (paradise fish) | 10°-32°C |
| | *M. cupanus dayi* | 15°-32°C |
| Cichlidae | Most species | 20°-27°C |
| | African Lake species | 23°-27°C |
| | *Hemichromis bimaculatus* (jewel fish) | 13°-32°C |
| | *Cichlasoma facetum* | 15°-27°C |

**Approximate temperature ranges of various families of fishes.**

Pristellas, *Pristella maxillaris* (above), lemon tetras, *Hyphessobrycon pulchripinnis* (top, opposite page), and black tetras, *Gymnocorymbus ternetzi* (bottom, opposite page), are easy to keep and breed. The fancy variety of black tetra shown has very long fins and will require a bigger tank.

In temperate areas, garden pool owners often prefer to drain their pools during winter rather than keep fish, if any, outdoors. However, the usual garden pool fishes (goldfish and koi or Japanese colored carp) can survive and possibly breed in early spring.

white spot or ich, which is caused by an organism frequently present in the water but which does not usually gain a hold in healthy fishes. The usual symptoms of heat shock are gasping respiration, surface hugging, and sometimes lack of balance, so that the fish turns slowly onto its side, plunges to an upright position, and then repeats the process.

The above discussion applies to adult fishes. Their eggs and fry are usually much tougher and can stand a greater variability and a wider range of temperature than their parents. As the young fishes grow up, this tolerance is gradually lost. It also applies to involuntary changes which the fishes cannot avoid. In a pool or a tank, the water may be stratified, with quite large differences in temperature between top and bottom. The free swimming of fishes from one layer to another in these conditions is not harmful, probably because they do not stay long at any one fixed temperature and can tolerate short periods of immersion in hotter or colder strata. A day-to-night fluctuation in average temperature of 3° to 4°C is also safe for most freshwater fishes but *not* for many marine or estuarine types. A fluctuation of 5° to 8°C is dangerous and a common cause of otherwise unexplained trouble.

Books on aquarium fishes frequently list odd tolerance ranges such as 68° to 75°F simply because they are derived from European continental references which are in degrees Centigrade. Their most common low temperature is 20°C, which is 68°F; a temperature of 24°C is 75°F. The commonest range of perfectly tolerable temperature for tropicals is 20° to 27°C, but variations from this are known to be acceptable for various "old favorites" whose adaptability has been well tested. Most tropical fishes are uncomfortable above or below this range, particularly below it. They are mostly in danger if much below 20°C but not in severe danger above 27°C, unless it is prolonged for many days or the fishes are crowded.

The temperatures above are mostly *not* the temperature range for breeding, which is usually but not always toward the upper part of the range, or at any rate above 24°C. Exceptions are most Cyprinidae, *Corydoras*, *Oryzias latipes*, and *Macropodus opercularis*. Breeding in very large tanks or ponds will often occur at lower temperatures.

The breeding tank setup should suit the spawning behavior of your fish. The Sumatra barb, *Capoeta tetrazona* (above), is an egg-scatterer that requires a well-planted aquarium, while the jewelfish, *Hemichromis bimaculatus* (below), needs an exposed flat surface.

In its natural habitat the Argentine pearlfish, *Cynolebias bellottii*, spawns in soft mud each year during the rainy season. For breeding this species in the tank, hobbyists sometimes use a synthetic spawning grass instead of the traditional peat moss.

The firemouth cichlid, *Cichlasoma meeki,* frequently spawns in a cave-like arrangement in a tank that is guarded closely from intruders.

# REPRODUCTION

Details of fish reproduction will be dealt with in the relevant later chapters, and remarks here are confined to a few general principles.

The sexes are always separate in freshwater fishes kept in the aquarium, and, in the few cases in which it has been studied, sex determination is genetic, as in other vertebrates. Unlike most other vertebrates, however, the genetic sex may sometimes alter spontaneously, particularly in livebearers. When this occurs, the transformation is usually from female to male. Winge, who has studied the guppy extensively, has shown that it is possible to swing sex determination from one pair of chromosomes to another, so that this mechanism in the live-bearers would seem to be in a primitive state.

Fertilization is usually external, at the moment of spawning, and fish sperm do not live long once they have been ejected into the water (about 60 seconds in the case of the trout). Some aquarium fishes are community spawners, such as most *Rasbora* species, but the majority will spawn in single pairs, even though in nature they may spawn communally.

The fertilized eggs usually hatch rapidly. Those of many characins hatch within 24 hours at about 24° to 27°C, most barbs within 40 hours, and goldfish in about three days at 27°C but as long as a week at 15°C. Panchax varieties take 10 to 14 days, and, at the other extreme, the eggs of some of the annual killies such as *Nothobranchius* may take several months. The young are usually very small and require careful and special feeding, excepting larger young, such as those of most live-bearers. Typical numbers of eggs per spawning are 100 to 1,000 in aquarium species, most of which should be fertile. This contrasts sharply with species like the cod, which lays some 9,000,000 eggs. Live-bearers drop anything from half a dozen to 200 young, the larger numbers only from older females.

There are persistent reports that particular strains or species produce a great preponderance of one sex. The local strain of *Capoeta titteya* in Sydney, Australia, was once agreed to produce anything from 90 to 99% females, and it was therefore some surprise that a purchase of six turned out to be all males. Very great

The functional copulatory organ (gonopodium) of the male poecilid is seen clearly in this photo of *Phallichthys amates,* a well-known livebearer rarely seen in the hobby today.

During a typical poecilid courtship, as in *Heterandria formosa* seen here, the male pursues the female from behind and directs the gonopodium forward, ready for insertion.

The elephant nose, *Gnathonemus petersi,* has attracted some aquarists because of its interesting feeding habit of probing the bottom with its snout. However, this species is not known to breed in captivity.

The clown loach, *Botia macracantha,* is the most attractive and most popular of the cobitids.

Discus, *Symphysodon,* are beautiful fishes for a display tank. They are peaceful and when maintained in good tank conditions and free of parasites survive well and can breed in captivity.

caution is necessary before such opinions are accepted, because, unless the whole of a spawning is preserved until it can be sexed, there is the likelihood that the method used for culling selectively eliminates more or nearly all of one particular sex. This will be particularly likely if there is a sex difference in, say, size or in brightness of color, and the unwary owner culls the apparent runts and duller fish. A spawning of glowlights (*Hemigrammus erythrozonus*) was neatly divided into practically equal groups of males and females, when the intention was to throw out the less well-developed fishes (males). There is, in fact, every reason to suppose that about equal numbers of males and females will normally be produced, although it is quite possible for there to be a differential death rate during growth.

Exceptions occur in some of the killifishes, whose eggs hatch usually only after a period of drying. In these, a first hatch may produce a preponderance of one sex, but if the remaining unhatched eggs are redried a preponderance of the opposite sex may appear on second hatching.

There is also a common prejudice against early breeding, and it is even sometimes recommended that a fish like the glowlight should not be spawned before it is two years old. There seems to be no good reason for this. Early spawning may not yield as many eggs, but it certainly does not seem to impair later fertility or fecundity in any way. In fact, it is the writer's experience that early, frequent spawning is the way to get the more "difficult" species trained to their job. Typical records for young pairs are the following, taken from a pair of Sumatra barbs (*Capoeta tetrazona*):

| First spawning | 40 young at 6 weeks |
| Second spawning | 62 young at 6 weeks |
| Third spawning | 325 young at 6 weeks |

The spawnings were at two-week intervals.

# CHAPTER THREE

## Feeding Fishes

Since fish farming has become a significant industry, and the preparation of dry foods for aquarium fishes has been the subject of more research than previously, we do know more than we did a decade or two ago. It turns out that fishes are remarkably good converters of food into fish, even of vegetable food. The brown trout converts over 50% of commercial feedstuffs into itself, whereas a typical wild animal would convert no more than about 10%, domestic animals up to about 30% at best. Chickens are its nearest rival, at about 35% conversion. However, many fish do even better on a high-protein diet, which is the reason that the protein content of foods as listed on the packet is so important. It should not fall below 45-50% in dried, freeze-dried or flake foods. Older fishes can stand a lower protein content than young ones, but still require plenty, especially for breeding. The protein requirements also vary with water temperature, thus Chinook salmon needed 40% at 8 °C, rising to 55% at 14.5 °C in one experiment, to produce the same weight gain. Marine fishes require more protein—at least 55% in some instances, and fishes such as trout require more protein the higher the salinity of the water. Other important constituents of a fish diet are carbohydrates and fats. Starch as such is indigestible and needs to be broken down, and simple sugars are best utilized by fishes. Fats are a ready source of energy, but animal fats (saturated fats) cannot be digested by at least some fishes. The fat of fishes is polyunsaturated, oily and is best fed in that form. Maximum growth is said to be achieved with the longer chain polyunsaturated fats ($C_{22}$ or $C_{24}$).

Vitamin requirements of fish still need further study, but the water-soluble vitamins appear to function much the same as in higher vertebrates. Among the B vitamins, tocopherols are needed in particular to assist fat assimilation, thiamine to assist with carbohydrate utilization and pyridoxine requirements are related to

Guppies, *Poecilia reticulata,* are attractive and very prolific. However, the development of a uniform strain is difficult to achieve without a careful and well documented breeding program.

The chief attraction of "kissing gouramis," *Helostoma temmincki,* is their tendency to lock the lips together.

The male American flagfish, *Jordanella floridae,* is more colorful than the female, especially during breeding when more red appears on the body.

This shell-dwelling African mbuna import, *Pseudotropheus lanisticola*, is of particular interest to African cichlid enthusiasts. Without a shell, the fish feels threatened. A new larger shell is introduced to replace the smaller outgrown shell.

protein intake and thus needed more in carnivorous fishes. The requirement for vitamin C (ascorbic acid) is, as in other animals which need it at all, related to stress, growth rate and rate of healing. Many animals can make their own vitamin C, but at least some fishes cannot. Fat-soluble vitamins have not been well studied, despite their concentration in fish liver oils. It does not seem to be known whether vitamins A and D are essential to most fishes, but an excess of either in the diet has been reported as harmful. Also, in trout, vitamin $D_3$ is needed for calcium uptake.

Little is also known about mineral requirements, although it must be necessary for adequate amounts of calcium and phosphorus to be available in the diet of freshwater fishes for bone growth. Iodine deficiency has been reported in trout, with resultant thyroid gland disturbances. Also in trout, magnesium is necessary for adequate growth and kidney function, and there must be a balance in the intake of magnesium, calcium and phosphorus—just as in mammals.

These facts are of little practical importance as long as we can supply natural food to the fishes. Too often we cannot, and then it is desirable to supply as near a copy as we can or to substitute foods which have been shown by experience to produce satisfactory results. The requirements may be different for breeding from those needed for mere healthy maintenance in a community tank.

## NATURAL FOODS

Nearly all fry feed on plankton, which consists of single-celled organisms (infusoria), insects in young stages, crustaceans, and worms and other water creatures, or even other young fishes. The size of the food they eat depends on their own size and mouth capacity. Very small fry in the early stages consume the smallest single-celled algae and ciliates, graduating later to the larger single-celled animals and plants and then to multi-celled creatures. Such fry are those of the Siamese fighting fish (*Betta splendens*) and many other anabantids. Larger fry, such as those of the barbs, can start further up the scale.

Older fishes vary more in their natural foods, and many have a considerable omnivorous capacity.

The natural food of the brooktrout, by now obvious to the reader as one of the very few fishes studied in detail, has been found to be 89% insects, 8% crustaceans and 3% other fishes or mollusks. This diet gives 49% protein and 15% fat. The rest is carbohydrate and a lot of non-digestible chitin from the insects and crustaceans.

*Characins* are mostly carnivorous and feed on insects, crustaceans, snails and other mollusks, or on other fishes small enough to be swallowed. Some eat vegetable matter by choice, such as *Hemigrammus caudovittatus*, and many will eat it if they have to do so.

*Cyprinids* are omnivorous, taking both animal and vegetable food, with a preference for the former if they can get it. Many get along quite well with little but vegetables, however, particularly the carps and the barbs. A survey of the food of Indian barbs showed that algae and diatoms (small, shelled plants) formed their main diet, although in five of the nine species studied crustaceans were also eaten. In the aquarium, these same fishes would probably get along better with meatier food.

*Cyprinodonts* feed mostly on surface insects, crustaceans, worms, fry, and other fishes. They will eat dead vegetable food only if they have no choice, and the extent to which they do this in nature is not reported.

*Poeciliids* like algae and other water plants, and they also like practically anything else. They seem, however, to need a supply of live vegetable food for best health and reproduction.

*Cichlids, anabantids,* and practically all the rest of the aquarium fishes are carnivorous by preference and omnivorous by necessity. Some gouramis need algae—the kissing gourami (*Helostoma temmincki*) in particular. The larger members of these families are particularly likely to be carnivorous and predatory—i.e., active seekers and eaters of living animals, including other fishes.

Most of the above freshwater fishes can become accustomed to very different foods from those obtained naturally and thus can be successfully kept or reared in the home aquarium. Others are more choosy and will not readily learn to eat dried food or even dead food. They are fortunately rather few, but include *Badis badis*, some of the sticklebacks, and *Belonesox belizanus*.

Oscars, *Astronotus ocellatus,* of breeding size or older are fairly large fish and will require a large tank. They are not usually kept with smaller fishes for they will surely eat them. Oscars become tame and seem to be aware of their keeper.

**Opposite page:** Juvenile oscars show a marbled pattern (top) that becomes transformed to the pattern characteristic of adults of the species (bottom).

## MANUFACTURED FOODS

A very large choice of commercially made fish foods is now available, with some varieties specially designed to bring fishes into breeding condition. They are sometimes colored to attract the customer rather than the fishes, but this does not matter as long as the coloring matter is not harmful. Others may contain attractants, such as dried blood, which do stimulate feeding and are therefore of real value. Many containers specify the nature of the ingredients and the percentages of protein, fat and such found on analysis, and it is perhaps advisable to restrict purchases to those that do. The average good fish food contains 40% or 50% protein, for example, although special foods for vegetable eaters will necessarily fall short of this.

For all but large fishes, flake foods, made by drying thin layers of prepared mix over rollers, are very popular and can be used with many fishes as a staple diet, to be supplemented however with occasional feeds of some other kinds—including live or frozen foods. Flakes float on the water, where fishes soon learn to eat them, and may also drop gently down if left uneaten for a period. A good flake does not cloud the water or cause pollution if not eaten immediately, so that some can be left for later consumption—not too much though! No food should be left to accumulate for long, as it will decompose and pollute the tank in the end.

Granular dried foods can contain ingredients unsuited to turning into flakes and are better for the larger fishes, but in the right grain size they are still suitable for small ones. They may contain all kinds of suitable-sounding ingredients—ground insects, dried daphnia, fish roe, tuna flesh, meat, wheat meal, spinach, dried algae, egg and so forth—and are varied in composition to suit predominantly carnivorous or vegetarian fishes. As with color, one suspects that the nature of the ingredients, except for predominance of animal or vegetable material, attracts the aquarist rather than his fishes, although some fishes show preferences. Powdery varieties of these foods are suitable for young live-bearers at birth and for some types of fry. There is a tendency for manufacturers to offer less expensive and usually less nutritious foods for really large fishes such as carp and pond

74

fishes in general, but their needs are just the same as those of smaller fishes and their food should be as good. A large dog needs the same meat as a small one and would do very poorly on a diet of roughage and scraps!

Dried or freeze-dried but otherwise unprocessed single foods are also readily available—daphnia, tubifex, fairy shrimp, and of course the hoary old favorite "ants' eggs," which are in fact the pupae of ants and not very nutritious. Some of these foods, in particular the freeze-dried varieties, are very much appreciated by the fishes and would seem to be good value for the money. Freeze-dried tubifex worms, unfortunately not admitted to all countries, are a great favorite with the fishes and seem to be a good source of nutrition, likewise freeze-dried adult brine shrimp. The process of freeze-drying is stated to kill harmful bacteria, of especial importance with tubifex, but this seems unlikely. In any case, the bacteria are not dead when feeding ordinary live tubifex, so that as long as the worms do not still have a gut full of filth it probably doesn't matter very much.

## DEEP FROZEN OR CANNED FOODS

Many deep frozen, sometimes sterilized, foods are now available, covering even a greater range than the freeze-dried or dried products, as some natural foods are not readily dried successfully. A very good, in fact staple, diet can also be constructed from items intended for human consumption, such as deep frozen scallop, shrimp or prawns, fish itself of various types, and canned crab, lobster, spinach, peas and other vegetables, after grinding or chopping to sizes suitable to the fishes in question. For the more vegetarian fishes can be added breakfast cereals of suitable types—not sugar-frosted however!

A mix can be made, sieved and washed so as to get rid of unwanted fine particles and juices, then frozen and kept in suitable containers in the deep freeze compartment of a domestic refrigerator, where it will last almost indefinitely. Take out a day's feed at a time by using a suitable sized ice cube or similar tray so that you do not have to thaw and refreeze more than is required. The original purchases and the contents of opened cans should be placed in small plastic bags or containers and kept frozen for further use.

Fish imports from Africa often include the Malawi golden cichlid, *Melanochromis auratus*, a mouthbrooder that breeds well in aquarium conditions. This cichlid is also bred today in Florida for the American market. The lower side of the male's body becomes very dark during breeding.

A small school of dwarf pencilfish, *Nannostomus marginatus*, fits well in a community tank. Domestically raised populations of many species of pencilfishes accept dry food.

The kribensis, *Pelvicachromis pulcher*, is a good-looking fish with a beautiful pattern and bright coloration.

The author has fed both freshwater and marine fishes exclusively on such a diet for months on end, as an experiment, with quite satisfactory results. If you feel like it, *small* amounts of a multi-vitamin preparation can be added to the original mix, but it doesn't seem necessary. Two typical multi-vitamin capsules per kilo of food, very carefully mixed in so as not to give an alarming and possibly harmful dose in one part of the food, is about right. Alternatively, suitable vitamin-containing preparations can be purchased which are intended for aquarium use. Use very sparingly, since if one drop per 5 liters is recommended for adding periodically to the whole tank, from which the fishes will absorb very little vitamin, it is clear that more than a drop or two per kilo of food will be excessive.

Another way of dealing with preserved or canned foods is to make a paste of them as originally recommended by Myron Gordon. His original mix, obviously intended for feeding very large numbers of fishes (which is not surprising since he kept about 600 aquaria) was as follows:

| | |
|---|---|
| Beef liver | 5 lb |
| Pablum or Ceravim | 14 lb |
| Shrimp shell meal | 6 lb |
| Shredded shrimp meat | 3 lb |
| Spinach | 3 lb |

The raw beef liver is cut into 5 cm pieces and boiled for 15 minutes, then ground or chopped to a suitable size. The water in which it was boiled is used to boil up the rest of the formula, the chopped liver is returned to the mix for a further 15 minutes' boiling, and the paste is ground and kept for feeding, *or* it can be frozen and fed as a paste. It is of course perfectly possible to make smaller quantities of Gordon's formula—substitute 1 oz or 30 gm for lb, for example.

For feeding fry, fine food may be made from coarser supplies by grinding them in a pepper mill or by crushing them between flat tiles and then sieving carefully. Such food for young fishes preferably contains more animal material and may be made from 100% dried shrimp or crab.

It is a frequent practice to float a "feeding ring" on the surface of the water when using dried food. This is a small ring of hollow glass or plastic which confines the food to a portion of the tank and makes it easier to remove unconsumed portions.

## OTHER PREPARED FOODS

Most fishes like the various baby foods or cereals. They may be made as for human consumption, but preferably with a little dried shrimp mixed in. Serve it in small soggy lumps and expect to have to clear up the tank afterwards unless you gauge the fishes' appetites very precisely.

The cold-water fishes, mostly heavy eaters, are particularly fond of chopped-up canned foods and may conveniently be fed frequently on them. Ham, chopped to a suitable size, is particularly recommended by some Continental breeders as a suitable substitute for live foods. The fishes may have to learn to like it, but once they have done so it is greedily eaten, even by tropicals which normally eat only live foods.

Fishes also eat egg in various forms—as an omelette, boiled and chopped up, or poured into boiling water and beaten as it solidifies. They readily eat meat, particularly minced heart or liver, but this should be fed only occasionally, as it seems to produce intestinal troubles if used too much, resulting in thin fishes and fouled tanks. Fishes fed on heart alone do not thrive, and it has been shown to possess a toxic factor. Goldfish may be fed almost anything from the kitchen that is not spiced or oily—because the oil spreads as a film over the water, not because it is indigestible or otherwise harmful—but any food must be fresh and of suitable size. Finally, fishes like fish, fresh, cut up or minced, or boiled and shredded. However, too much raw fish has vitamin-destroying properties and should be avoided.

## LIVE FOODS

The conscientious aquarist who likes to keep his fishes in the best of health and who wants to breed them frequently probably spends as much time in collecting and culturing live foods as on anything else. Only a very fortunate man can obtain as much as he really feels his fishes need, particularly in winter and particularly if he lives in a town and keeps many fishes. Live foods

**Left:** Almost any fish will eat tubifex worms, but they should be given with care and cleaned well for they sometimes carry parasites and diseases. **Below:** Many aquarists feel that mosquito larvae are a good natural food for fishes. Unfortunately, they are not available throughout the year and also are not found in some parts of the country.

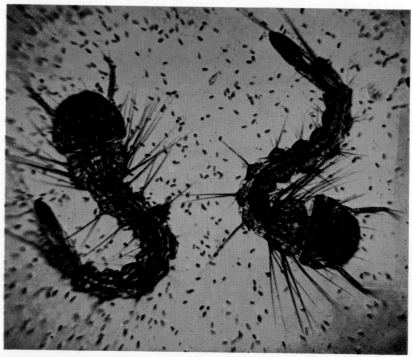

**Right:** Newly hatched nauplii of brine shrimp, *Artemia salina,* are suitable for very tiny fishes and fish fry. **Below:** A swarm of adult brine shrimp. The dark structures present in some individuals are egg sacs of females.

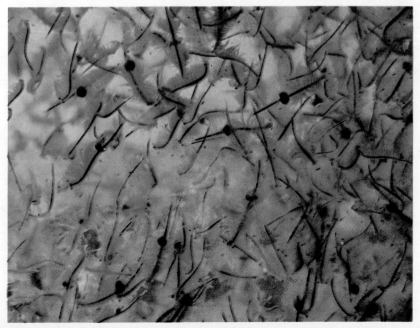

are not absolutely essential for all species, but they are always desirable, and breeding is unlikely without them except in the live-bearers and a few hardy egg-layers. The spirit and appearance, to say nothing of growth rate, of fishes reared entirely on such prepared foods as are at present available leave much to be desired in the great majority of cases. On the other hand, entirely live diets are quite unnecessary except in the few instances where the fishes won't eat prepared food. Something in the neighborhood of 40 to 50% of live food seems to give as good results as 100%, and, if an attempt to feed only live food means reduced rations, fish on prepared food may do better.

## Earthworms

The *earthworm* holds an important place as a live food, being practically always available. It is a fine fish food, given whole to the big fishes, chopped to the smaller ones, and shredded to the very small ones or to fry. Special shredders may be purchased, resembling a pair of small phonograph records. The worm is placed between shredders, which are rubbed across each other with a brisk rotary motion, with worm puree as the result. If you are sensitive, the worms can be killed immediately before use by plunging them into hot water. Unfortunately, fishes seem to prefer them uncooked. Earthworms may be stored in leaf mold or in urban shrub boxes or window boxes, and they may be coaxed from the lawn by pouring a solution of potassium permanganate at a strength of about 4 mg per liter onto the surface. They emerge in a few minutes. Avoid the dung worm, which is yellow and smelly and not good for fishes.

## Insect Larvae

Insect larvae are another fine live food. Those of various species of mosquitos and gnats are the easiest to collect in the right circumstances and may be netted in thousands in warm weather from stagnant water. They can be purposely cultivated by leaving suitable receptacles in the garden, but it is important to avoid increasing the adult mosquito population. For such collecting, it is important to have smelly, stagnant, dirty water. Clean water offers little food and does not attract the female mosquito. Decaying leaves or even meat will attract her.

The female lays eggs rafts, small sooty-looking floating masses of 200 to 300 eggs, which hatch out into a swarm of minute "wrigglers." Typical species develop through the next 8 or 9 days and then hatch, offering a nice range of sizes for fish food. The larvae grow steadily and molt several times, finally turning into comma-shaped pupae which soon hatch into adults. The larvae and pupae are air-breathers and so may be fed freely to the fishes without fear of crowding them out, although there is the possibility of their hatching into adults if given in excess.

When collecting larvae or pupae, it is best to catch them as cleanly as possible with a fine net and then, if necessary, to sort them for size by letting them wriggle down through a sieve or series of sieves made from various meshes of wire screening. If they are to be transported any distance they may die from overcrowding. This can be avoided by making a cabinet with shallow shelves lined with wet cloth, or by a series of grids so lined. If kept moist, the larvae will survive for many hours. If they are stored in a refrigerator, they keep longer without metamorphosis and also keep sweeter. It is advisable to wash catches thoroughly and to feed the bigger ones only to fishes large enough to eat any unwanted young predators as well. Care must of course be taken to exclude any sizable insect larvae, such as those of the dragonfly, likely to escape being eaten and to grow to dangerous proportions.

*Chironomus* larvae (bloodworms) are rather similar but are bloodred. Their parents are also gnats. They tend to stay down more than other gnat or mosquito larvae and must be separated from mud after collection. This is best done by sieving, as with the others, choosing a mesh so that the mud escapes and the larvae are retained. Alternatively, they may be siphoned from jars, leaving most or all of the mud behind. After shaking the mud with contained larvae, it is allowed to settle, and the larvae are left behind for a short period as the mud falls down.

*Chaoborus* larvae (glassworms) are like bloodless *Chironomus* larvae, but they are found in cold weather and swim freely in the water. Sometimes they may be collected in quantity, and they keep well in crowded conditions. (Note that the terms "bloodworms" and "glassworms" are misnomers—the creatures are insect larvae.)

*Maggots* of various types are readily taken by the larger fishes.

The most common variety of the three-spot gourami, *Trichogaster trichopterus*, is the blue variety.

The golden strain of *Trichogaster trichopterus* was developed in East Germany. Except for their color, the pattern of the body and the fin markings are not different from the common variety.

Their culture is not usually a welcome proposition, but in localities where garbage accumulates undisturbed a large number may sometimes be collected. Maggots are not suitable for chopping up. Other insect larvae are rarely collected in sufficient quantities to matter, but a mixed bag of the harder shelled types— those of water boatmen, for instance—are welcomed by large fishes like the cichlids and most anabantids.

## Crustaceans

The Crustacea provide many popular live foods, the chief of which is *Daphnia pulex*, the water flea. These small crustaceans are about the size of fleas and appear in warm, but not hot, weather, in stagnant pools. They may be almost colorless, green, or red, depending on the variety and also on their food. The red ones have hemoglobin, the same blood pigment we have.

When really plentiful, *Daphnia* occurs in large clouds and may be netted out in thick clumps, so thick that an improperly shaped net will ball them up together and injure them. The right net is fairly shallow and does not come to a point at the bottom but is rounded. The fleas will suffocate if not given fair room during transportation, and they should also be kept cool. It is not easy to keep them alive in layers of cloth as for mosquito larvae.

For some reason, *Daphnia* is regarded by many as the food *par excellence*. It is not actually very good food value, as it has a high water content and a hard, tough shell, and fishes fed exclusively on it do not thrive as a rule. It should be used in moderation for most tropical fishes, but it may be fed more liberally (when available!) to goldfish. It is available in dried form but is rather expensive this way, except for the fact that the dried eggs in the bodies of the females will often hatch out and can be used to start a live *Daphnia* culture. These are the winter eggs, which normally last over winter and hatch out the following spring.

The artificial cultivation of *Daphnia* is possible on quite a big scale, if large pools are available, and on a worthwhile scale even in tubs or old tanks. The crustaceans normally live on unicellular algae and other organisms, and these must be supplied in bulk. They are cultured by enriching the water in the pool or tub with decaying vegetable matter or manure. Sheep manure is said to be best. An appropriate pool would be, say 1.5 x 2.0 meters in area and 0.5 meter deep. After it is liberally seeded with refuse, the *Daphnia* are introduced and should breed well. Such a pool might yield enough *Daphnia* to feed several hundred small fishes two or three times a week, but don't expect too much. Indoors, such procedures are smelly, and yeast or wheat flour may be used as the source of nourishment instead. If kept well aerated, these concoctions have little or no smell.

*Moina, Cyclops, Diaptomus*, and other less important Crustacea are found in the same fashion as *Daphnia* and can also be cultivated. They are not usually so abundant, nor are they as palatable to all fishes, but they are small and easily cultivated, and growing fry welcome them. *Cyclops*, unfortunately, seems to feed on the unhatched eggs of tropicals and should be excluded from breeding tanks at the initial stage.

*Gammarus* species and *Asellus* species are two common larger crustaceans. They are both 1 to 2 cm in length, and both can be cultured in conditions similar to those for *Daphnia*. They are caught in the roots of border plants and rushes and often occur in streams. They are eagerly taken by the larger fishes, and their younger stages are eaten by smaller species. They have also the advantage that they survive for an appreciable period in salt water and so may be fed to 'marine fishes. Uneaten specimens—and it is surprising how long *Gammarus*, in particular, sometimes manages to escape—are excellent scavengers. Another useful freshwater crustacean is *Hyalella*, which is also easy to raise and has the advantage over *Gammarus* and *Asellus* that it will stand tropical heat for breeding.

## Brine Shrimp

The brine shrimp, *Artemia salina*, is also a crustacean, but it merits a heading to itself. It is a live food of growing importance, in more senses of the word than one, as without it thousands of young fishes would never reach maturity. The genus *Artemia* is composed of small shrimps which live in very salty water, such as the Great Salt Lake in Utah, and whose eggs can withstand drying up completely for many years. Hence it is very important, for these eggs are now collected commercially and made available to aquarists all over the world. They can be stored for over a decade if necessary, as long as they are kept dry and at an even

The color pattern of the convict cichlid, *Cichlasoma nigrofasciatum*, is variable. The body stripes can vary in number and intensity from the young stages to the adult.

The "pink" convict is just as easy to breed as the regular convict cichlid. Both are regularly available in most aquarium shops.

A Malawi blue cichlid or zebra, *Pseudotropheus zebra,* photographed in its natural habitat. Its natural diet consists of small animals and algae found on the rocks on the shores of Lake Malawi.

One of the very many varieties (morphs) of the blue cichlid found in its natural habitat is the mottled morph. Different morphs can interbreed in captivity and produce offspring of diverse color patterns.

temperature. More remarkable still, they can be dried out again, even after they have become moist, and they still will retain their hatching capacity.

The eggs look like a fine brown powder and are very minute. About the smallest pinch you can take contains several hundred, and it is customary to hatch many thousands at a time. They are not used until they are hatched—it is the living young shrimp that are of importance in feeding baby fishes and even adults of the smaller species. There are two main methods of hatching, in shallow pans or in deep culture jars with aeration. San Francisco eggs may be hatched by either method, but Utah eggs seem to yield a higher proportion of young in aerated water.

The following directions apply principally to San Francisco eggs. The eggs hatch only in *salt* water, but oddly enough they hatch more quickly and more evenly in weaker salt water than is needed by the adults. They thrive beautifully in sea water, although the adults do not. Thus, for hatching, use six heaped tablespoons of salt to 4 liters of tap water (a 3½% salt solution). The eggs will float on the surface and should be sprinkled onto the water and left there, using not more than one teaspoon of eggs per 8 liters of water in shallow vessels. The eggs will hatch in about a day at temperatures of over 20 °C, but they will take a week or more at less than 18 °C. Even at 20 °C some of the eggs will take a couple of days to hatch out. If more eggs than recommended above are used, relatively fewer will hatch.

The empty egg shells will continue to float if undisturbed, whereas the shrimp swim in the body of the water with a jerky motion. They also collect in the most brightly lighted part of the vessel and will congregate so thickly that they will suffocate in a spot that is really bright in contrast to the rest. They may be siphoned off free of egg shells if the last few teaspoons of water are left behind, and then drained on an old handkerchief or other cloth. They should then be rinsed in fresh water to avoid introducing gradual doses of unwanted salt into the freshwater tank, and fed with an eye dropper or by rinsing the cloth in the tank. The hatching water may be used repeatedly as many as six times, replacing evaporated water with fresh tap water, as the salt doesn't evaporate.

In the alternative method of hatching, 4- or 5- liter jars, or even larger vessels, are two-thirds filled with the same salt water as above and subjected to brisk aeration. One or two teaspoons of eggs may then be used per 4 liters, and the eggs are whirled around in the water until they hatch. To collect the shrimp, the aeration is turned off and the eggs allowed to settle; this they usually do partly on the bottom and partly on the top. The shrimp may then be siphoned off with little or no egg shells. There are also special outfits on the market for the deep hatching of brine shrimp, with convenient taps for running them off from the base of the culture vessels.

Brine shrimp grow to about 1 cm in length and are a meaty meal at that stage. They need a different brine from that used in hatching, so newly hatched shrimp should be transferred within a day or two to a brine made by taking a cup (about 300 gm) of salt, two heaped tablespoons (60 gm) of Epsom salts, and one tablespoon of baking soda to 4 liters of tap water. This brine is about twice the strength of sea water and much more alkaline.

The young shrimp (*nauplii*) feed naturally on algae, etc., but bakers' yeast may be substituted—about ¼ teaspoon per 4 liters, well stirred up. Into 4 liters of brine plus yeast, preferably in a shallow tub or tray, put just a few shrimp—not more than a few hundred, unless you intend to use them only partially grown, in which case thousands can be reared. Feed yeast again when the brine clears, which may be in a day or a week, according to temperature and the number of shrimp. Cover to prevent too much evaporation. The shrimp reach maturity in about 6 weeks, sooner if kept really warm, and they will feed on yeast throughout the period and reproduce readily. Thus, the culture, if undisturbed, will soon contain both young and older shrimps, but do not expect it to yield an indefinite supply—you will still need to buy more eggs. Siphon off and wash the adults as you would the young before using them.

It is possible to purchase shell-less brine shrimp eggs, which can be placed directly into a saltwater aquarium and give a clean hatch, if not eaten directly. Otherwise, hatch as usual.

## Tubificid Worms

The mud worms or sludge worms, *Tubifex rivulorum* and other similar *Tubifex* or *Limnodrilus* species, are excellent food, but

Anybody with the slightest interest in the aquarium hobby must be aware of the zebra danio, *Brachydanio rerio,* the fish most often recommended by experienced hobbyists for beginners.

A long-finned variety of zebra danio is now available commercially. Breeders find this variety has a greater tendency for egg-binding (inability to expel the eggs).

During breeding, the male rosy barb, *Puntius conchonius,* attains a brilliant coloration never developed by the female.

A pair of the long-finned variety of rosy barb. In addition to a bushy plant, some artificial spawning grass has been added to trap the eggs during spawning.

they are found in very questionable circumstances and should be carefully washed before use. Tubifex worms absorb waste material from slow-moving polluted streams, being rarely found in quantity in stagnant water. They are reddish in color and vary with species from threadlike creatures 2 to 5 cm long to really solid worms 8 to 10 cm in length. They live at the bottom or sides of streams and wave their tails in the water, retiring promptly into a tube in the mud when disturbed. They may establish themselves in an aquarium and be hard to eliminate (*Corydoras* do this), and whether they are regarded as an acquisition or a nuisance depends on the aquarist.

Collecting Tubifex is usually a filthy task. If they are present in worthwhile amounts they will be seen as a reddish wriggling carpet or patches which jerk into the mud when a shadow or footfall disturbs them. Dig well under the mud where a patch was seen—or if you are lucky the patch may be so thick that even when retracted it is still visible—and put mud and all into a large bucket. When you have a bucket nearly full, leave it until lack of oxygen forces the worms to collect at the surface, when they may be removed with some mud still adhering to them. If they must be left for long, run a gentle drip of water into the bucket and if possible cover with a layer of sand, through which they will emerge fairly clean. Otherwise they will die and be useless. Most of the worms can be removed within a day or two. Wash the worms well under a fairly brisk stream of water to remove much of the residual mud. They will aggregate into balls and may be stored for a long time, even a month, if they are placed in large vessels of water under a constant drip from a tap or hose, with a suitable overflow arrangement. They also store well in an ice chest or refrigerator, and clear of mud they do not smell until they start to die. Stored masses should occasionally be stirred up and washed more briskly to remove the dead and the feces, and they should not be fed to fishes for at least the first day.

Tubifex may be cultivated in slowly fed muddy streams, artificially made in the garden, but it is not an easy task and the arrangement is unsightly. They will live on stale bread broken up and thrust into the mud, but they really thrive only in filthier conditions than the most ardent fan is likely to tolerate. A word of warning—do not wash and prepare your tubifex in the kitchen sink or even at an adjacent drain which communicates with it. They have a remarkable facility for collecting in U-bends, where they feed on waste from the domestic washing-up, etc., and eventually cause blockage.

## White Worms

White worms (enchytraeids) are relatives of tubifex and of the earthworms. They are small worms about 2.5 cm in length, commonly found in cool, moist surroundings where there is plenty of humus or other decaying matter for them to use as food. The underside of garbage containers when on soil is a favorite spot, but the worms are practically never collected from such sites now, as they may be purchased from dealers to start a culture. The common variety is *Enchytraeus albidus*.

There are several methods for cultivating them. They may be cultured on a fair scale in wooden boxes of rich soil with added humus and oatmeal. These are stored in cool cellars, and more oatmeal, mashed potatoes, cheese, bread, and milk or a variety of other foods are placed on the soil or into small holes in it at intervals of a few days. The box is tightly covered, preferably by a sheet of glass in contact with the top of the soil, mainly to exclude ants and other predators (even mice), but also to keep a damp state—not wet, just damp. When needed, the worms may be scraped off the glass or from the food pockets.

On a smaller scale, the worms may be cultured between milk-soaked crusts of bread stored in tightly covered tins or other vessels. It is advisable to boil the milk and to pour it on the crusts while hot, as this helps to sterilize them and to prevent early souring of the culture. This method nevertheless requires frequent sub-culturing, as the bread slices rapidly go foul and moldy.

There is usually little trouble in separating white worms from their food, but if necessary, place the mass of half-cleaned worms on a rather hot surface and they will rapidly crawl to the top.

## Microworms

This is a group of minute nematode worms of the genus *Anguillula*, the most familiar being the vinegar eel, *A. aceti*, and the paste eel, *A. glutinis*. Another, *A. silusiae*, is found in soil, and it is assumed that this is the species usually called the

A black acara, *Aequidens portalegrensis,* female in the act of laying eggs on a smooth-surfaced rock that was cleaned earlier.

A male black acara guarding the spawn. Note the more distinct markings and intense coloration in comparison to those of the female (opposite page).

microworm. It was first cultivated by Swedish aquarists. It is a very small live-bearing worm, at a maximum about 0.25 cm long, with young very much smaller. Therefore it is an important food for young fishes, and it is beginning to rival brine shrimp as it is considerably cheaper to cultivate in large amounts and the younger stages are smaller than newly hatched brine shrimp.

The microworm is easy to culture. This is best done in shallow vessels with tight covers. In the base of each vessel is placed about a 0.5 cm layer of any of the quick-cooking breakfast oatmeals or wheatmeals. The use of wheat germ is said to give superior results. The meal is cooked just as for ordinary use, preferably with milk, but without salt. It is then inoculated with a little bakers' yeast and some microworms. Alternatively, uncooked fine baby pablum may be used exactly as it is, with or without yeast, and wetted with water. It seems to give equally good results. Growth is rapid, and the worms form a seething mass in a few days. If small pieces of wood, water-soaked beforehand, are placed criss-cross over the meal so that the top ones are clear of it, the worms crawl up and collect, free of cereal, on the top pieces. If the sides of the vessel are roughened, as can be done with plastic containers, the worms will crawl up them and can be scraped off. It is not usually worthwhile to feed cultures once they have been established, but it is best to keep a series going so that worms are always ready for use. Each culture will last up to two weeks, and the worms thrive best in warm temperatures, up to 27 °C.

Microworms withstand desiccation, so that a dried-up culture can be restarted merely by wetting it.

## "Grindal" Worms

Another white worm, this one is intermediate in size between the usual one and the microworm. It was first cultivated by Mrs. Morten Grindal, a Swedish aquarist whose name has become attached to the worm. It was isolated from ordinary white worm cultures, and it prefers more heat than the usual enchytraeids. It is at most 1.25 cm in length and slimmer in proportion than white worms.

Culture may be in smaller vessels than for ordinary white worms and seems most successful when boiled peat is used rather than soil, humus, or bread. Pockets of food may be inserted into the peat, and this consists preferably of breakfast meals or pablum such as recommended for microworms. The food should be moist, not wet, and the culture should be kept from becoming too soggy. It may need repeated feeding at intervals of a few days, but should last for months before needing renewal. As before, a sheet of glass should be placed over the culture; the worms will congregate on and just below it. A temperature of 20° to 27°C is best.

## Infusoria and Algae

Microscopic pond life is legion, and much of it is suitable as food for fry. The word "infusoria" is so commonly used that it will be employed here, but it has lost any precise meaning except to denote anything very small in the way of pond animals, usually needing a microscope for recognition. The older German writers on aquatic matters were very fond of prescribing "pond infusoria" for the feeding of fry, with little hint of how hard it usually is to collect enough to be of any use. It is in any case much easier and safer to cultivate these organisms free of the unwanted pests and diseases which may be gathered in from the pond.

The rough-and-ready way—which usually produces quite satisfactory results—is to prepare a reasonably sterile medium and let it develop when exposed to the air. This will be made reasonably pleasant to the nose if aeration is supplied, and it also much improves the yield. A great variety of substances may form the base. The best is a rich vegetable infusion made by boiling almost anything from potato peelings to chopped lettuce leaves or banana skins for a few minutes and cooling. About a fistful per 40 liters is right. If you wish to cultivate a specific organism, keep the boiled water covered and introduce the desired species, either from a purchased culture or from a few specimens carefully selected by means of a fine pipette from pond water or another source. The infusoria appear in force within a few days. A temperature of 15° to 21°C is best, without too much light. In a strong light, an excess of algae is likely to develop, and this may swamp out the more desirable animal life. Single-celled free-swimming algae are useful, however, and are the cause of

One of the most common and popular dwarf cichlids bred for hobbyists is the ram, *Apistogramma ramirezi*. Unlike many typical cichlids, a dwarf cichlid is generally a very peaceful fish.

**Opposite page:** Another popular dwarf cichlid often seen in pet shops is *Apistogramma agassizi* (top). However, *Apistogramma amoenus* (bottom) is known mainly to a few breeders or aquarists who specialize in dwarf cichlids.

"green" water. These help to feed some of the infusoria, but if present in excess they may suddenly die and foul the culture.

There is little point in listing even the commonest forms of minute life found in such cultures. Particular attention has centered on a single-celled animal, *Paramecium*, and its value as a food, and on rotifers, multicellular but nevertheless small animals which are eaten by some fry as a next stage in the food cycle. These are only two of numerous common and, as far as we know, about equally valuable types. They or their eggs are capable of drying up and being carried in dust to suitable sites for further expansion. The success of a culture can be checked with a hand lens. Water taken from the lightest side of the vessel should swarm with life visible as moving specks in a drop placed on a glass slide and looked at against a dark background. Although infusoria are small, the useful ones are not so small that they cannot be seen in this manner, and anything that is too small to be visible with a simple lens is unlikely to be of much food value.

The vegetable infusion may be replaced by chemicals, but if this is done the first organisms to thrive in the culture will necessarily be algae, followed by animal life later. A suitable solution resembles those used in hydroponics, the water culture of higher plants. The constituents should be:—

| | |
|---|---|
| Potassium nitrate | 4 grams |
| Sodium chloride | 2 grams |
| Calcium sulphate | 2 grams |
| Magnesium sulphate | 2 grams |
| Calcium phosphate | 2 grams |

plus a trace of ferric chloride, in 4 liters of water.

## Fruit Fly

The vestigial wing mutation of *Drosophila melanogaster*, the fruit fly, is an offshoot of the genetic work done with this species. It is useful to aquarists because it cannot fly. It may be cultured in milk bottles with cotton wool plugs in the neck. The bottles are scalded and allowed to dry upside down and the sterile cotton wool plugs are placed in position. About one over-ripe banana per bottle is skinned, mashed, and sieved, and to the result is added 75 ml of water and ¼ teaspoon of nutrient agar per banana.

This is boiled over slow heat, with constant stirring, and when it is boiling ¼ teaspoon of mold inhibitor is added per banana; this will prevent the growth of unwanted molds. When it has been added, stirring is continued for three minutes and then about 2.5 cm of the liquid is poured into each bottle, leaving the neck open for as little time as possible. A small fan of sterile paper toweling, is also placed into each bottle, so that it reaches from the neck, below the plug, to the bottom. This is for the insects to crawl upon. Allow the bottles to cool, add a pinch of yeast, any variety, and a few flies. They will produce larvae in about a week and flies in about two weeks. They must be kept reasonably warm.

## Tadpoles and Fry

Newly hatched or half-grown tadpoles and fry of any fish are very good foods. Guppies, blue gouramis, and some of the barbs are particularly likely to overproduce; the egg-layers should be spawned when ripe, even if the fry are unwanted. They should be grown to a suitable size on prepared food if necessary and then fed to the more precious varieties. By this means, powdered food can be transformed to live food when the latter is in short supply. Take care, however, that the tables are not turned and that a rapidly growing, unconsumed gourami doesn't shoot ahead of its intended consumers and eat them instead.

## FEEDING

As explained in the preceding chapter, the warmer the water, the better the appetite of fishes, up to about 27 °C. Thus, goldfish need almost no feeding in the middle of winter and in normal cold weather should be fed only two or three times a week. In summer, however, twice daily is not too often. Tropicals are never so torpid as the coldwater varieties at the lower end of their temperature range but have in general poor appetites at temperatures below 20 °C. At 24 °C they are good eaters and should be fed two to three times daily, and at 27 °C they are really hungry and will eat practically as often as they are fed. Even so, they will not starve if fed only once per day, particularly if fed on live food, some of which may escape and be consumed later. Too much live food must not be given, however, or it may compete successfully for oxygen.

A strict vegetarian in its natural habitat, the Chinese algae-eater, *Gyrinocheilus aymonieri,* can keep a tank free of undesirable algal growth. It accepts dry food also.

*Belonesox belizanus* is one livebearer that requires a steady diet of small live fishes. Understandably, it is not recommended for the community tank.

A successful breeder of the butterfly fish, *Pantodon buchholzi,* recommends a diet of live insects, especially mosquito larvae, prior to breeding. He also declares that raising *Pantodon* is just as easy as raising young cichlids.

The feeding of prepared food requires careful handling. The tendency of the beginner is to give far too much. This is curious, as the true tyro often cherishes the belief that fishes live on microorganisms in the water and do not need feeding at all. From that, he seems to swing to the other extreme.

It is therefore more important than almost anything else in fish keeping that the following rule be *strictly adhered to at all times*. It is a rule given by Innes:

*Feed only enough prepared food at one time so that practically ALL of it is consumed within five minutes*. Then siphon off any that remains.

Only after long experience can an aquarist walk around his tanks and throw in the right amount of dry food without looking to see the result. Watch the fishes each time you feed them, see them eat the food, and see that they are well and alert and eating normally. Feed dried food fairly slowly, and give it time to swell up with water inside the fishes before they stuff themselves with too much. Some aquarists soak the food first, but the fishes do not usually eat it so readily when this is done. Feed little and often rather than the reverse.

As a rough guide, 1 ounce of prepared food such as a wheat germ and shrimp mixture will last 100 average-sized tropical aquarium fishes of mixed varieties at 24 °C for about two weeks with no other feeding. This is about 10 milligrams per fish per feeding, twice daily, which doesn't seem much but is enough.

As long as they are well fed normally, adult tropical fishes can be starved without trouble for several days. Even a couple of weeks is feasible, as long as the temperature is about 20 °C. Cold-water fishes can take starvation even more easily as long as they too are reasonably cool—say below 15 °C. Longer periods may be survived, but the tropicals at least will be pretty emaciated and may never breed again. The importance of this fact is that during a normal vacation of not more than two weeks it is possible to forget the fishes (not, of course, young fry). This may be preferable to getting someone else to feed them, unless he also is an aquarium keeper. Others nearly always manage to do something disastrous, the most common being gross overfeeding and pollution. If a non-fancier *must* be asked to undertake the task, it is vitally necessary to give him a few lessons or at least to make

106

Processed fish foods are available commercially in various weights and forms (freeze-dried, dehydrated, pelleted or flaked) to suit the convenience of hobbyists and the requirements of their fishes.

up separate packages of food, one per feeding, with strict instructions not to supplement them with anything else whatever. The latter method is perhaps the safer, with or without additional lessons! The remarkable thing is that a substitute can watch a tank go foul and cloudy, see fishes gasping at the surface, take out the dead ones, and still go on overfeeding.

The only food which can be given in mild excess to tide the fishes over a projected lean period is mosquito larvae. These do not consume dissolved oxygen to any appreciable extent and will survive if uneaten for several days on the average before turning into pupae and then adults. A tight cover over the tank will prevent the escape of any that manage to reach that stage. Only in a sparsely populated tank would it be worth risking the addition of substantial amounts of other live food, such as tubifex or white worms.

There are devices on the market for automatic feeding during the owner's absence which appear to work satisfactorily. There are also some new preparations which can be left in the aquarium to be nibbled away over a period of several days without fouling the water, but the author has no experience with them.

Cardinal tetras, *Cheirodon axelrodi* (above), and neon tetras, *Paracheirodon innesi* (below), may be small in size but they are popular on account of their brilliant coloration. To further enhance their beauty, they are displayed in large tanks with a dark bottom and background and are brightly lighted from above.

Congo tetras, *Phenacogrammus interruptus*, have rainbow-like iridescent scales and long fins. They are not aggressive, and several fish can be kept in a tank of the appropriate dimensions.

Guppy hobbyists are found all over the world today. Shown is a display tank of fancy guppies bred by Russian aquarists.

In addition to the common rectangular tanks, many pet shops today also have in their inventory of merchandise some odd-shaped tanks.

# CHAPTER FOUR

## The Principles of Aquarium Keeping

The construction of aquaria is an art in itself and, like the details of the various individual species of fish, will not be discussed in this volume. For most amateurs, it is cheaper in the long run to purchase suitable tanks than to make them, and generally it is more satisfactory. Aquaria for decorative purposes should be made from clear glass, without the irregularities and flaws frequent in ordinary window glass, and the glass should be thicker than window glass in any but the very smallest tanks. However, for aquaria less than 30 cm deep and 60 liters in capacity, it is not necessary to use plate glass for the sides, back, and front. These can be of 3 to 4 mm glass, with a 6 mm cast or plate glass bottom or a bottom of slate. Larger aquaria with a depth of up to 45 cm and a capacity of about 150 liters can be made of 6 mm plate or cast glass throughout. Above 150 liters and 45 cm in depth, thicker plate glass must be used; 9 mm plate with a 12 mm plate bottom is sufficient up to 400 liters and 60 cm in depth.

### SHAPE AND SIZE OF TANKS

Aquaria should be as shallow as possible, since the surface of the water exposed to the air is the most important factor determining the number of fishes they can safely hold. However, a very shallow tank is not decorative in most situations and a compromise is usual between biological and artistic requirements. Older tanks were simple "double cubes" with the tank twice as long as its height and width, e.g. 60 x 30 x 30 cm. This tank is still rather shallow and the modern trend, particularly with the common use of aeration, is to something such as 60 x 30 x 40 cm, the last being the height. The market offers anything from about

Angelfish, *Pterophyllum scalare* (silver variety, opposite page; marbled variety, above), are deep-bodied fish, and they should be maintained in tanks where it is possible for such fish to move freely.

113

25 x 15 x 20 cm upwards—even to tanks 240 cm long. This is a range of 8 liters to about 1000 liters.

Many other designs of tanks are of course possible. Hexagonal or other aquaria may fit nicely into a particular scheme. The main thing to remember is that a full tank needs very even, strong support. Most modern tanks are of all-glass construction and need to be sited on a resilient but firm pad of material such as styrofoam, which will accommodate small irregularities below and above itself. Older metal-framed tanks of any but the largest size can usually be supported along their front and back quite successfully, with no direct support for the glass or slate base.

Except for special purposes, small tanks are a mistake, as they give little scope for aquascaping, are vulnerable to temperature fluctuations, and hold few fishes. About the minimum useful size for an ordinary community tank is 45 x 20 x 25 cm (22.5 liters). To compute capacity in liters, multiply the length, breadth and height in cm together, and divide by 1,000, thus:

$$45 \text{ x } 20 \text{ x } 25 \text{ cm } = 22,500 \text{ cm}^3 = 22.5 \text{ liters.}$$

This refers to the actual volume of the tank (less glass thickness), and if allowances are made for a 2 cm air-space and 4 cm of gravel, the actual water volume is 17 liters approximately, perhaps further reduced by rocks.

## FISH CAPACITY OF TANKS

In Chapter One mention was made of the "balanced" aquarium and of the reciprocal actions of plants and animals. Until recently it was believed, however, that the exchange of carbon dioxide and oxygen between fish and plants, taking place directly through the water, was more important than is really the case. In a crowded tank, with plants in a good light, this interaction matters considerably, and the same tank is often in a poor state at night. With a tank not unduly crowded, either with fish or with plants, the exchange of gases between the air and water is more important than any other factor. This is why the *surface area* of the tank counts for so much and why, in practically all circumstances, the influence of plants may be ignored when fish capacity is considered from a respiratory point of view.

In addition to surface area, *surface movement* and the circulation of water within a tank are important, and that is why an aerated tank can hold more fishes than a still tank. The importance of movement and not of exchange between bubbles and the water is demonstrated by the surprising fact that aeration with pure carbon dioxide gas is successful in keeping fishes healthy. The fact that the movements of the water in normal aeration are produced by air bubbles is usually of little consequence, and it is an example of getting the right result for the wrong reason. The old idea behind aeration was, of course, to increase the contact of air and water by sending fine bubbles coursing up through the tank. Unless a very brisk spray of very fine bubbles is used, however, the surface of water exposed to air in the bubbles is small and unimportant, and the movement caused at the tank surface is what matters.

Thus, we compute fish capacity from surface area, and we may modify this by including the effects of temperature, water movement, and various other factors. The warmer the water, the lower the solubility of oxygen, and thus the lower the fish capacity. The following estimates assume an average temperature of about 24 °C for tropicals and about 15 °C for cold-water fishes. They assume no aeration, and they also assume that young fishes and small fishes, even though adult, use more oxygen per unit of body weight than do larger fishes. This is in line with such experimental details as are available, though they are scanty, and with general experience. They are *not* based on the old "gallon" or "inch of fish" rules, which give various estimates of the number of inches of fish per gallon which may be placed in tanks, because this type of computation is clearly fallacious and is not in line with either the practice or the experience of observant aquarists.

The general basis of the estimates is as follows. It is assumed that, age and activity apart, the same volume or weight of fish uses about the same amount of oxygen per minute, whether it comprises a hundred small fishes or one big fish. However, small fishes and young fishes are usually more active and young fishes are still rapidly growing. They therefore consume more oxygen weight for weight, and allowance is made for this to the extent that 1 gm of 1 cm fishes is allowed five times the oxygen con-

Monos, *Monodactylus argenteus,* are coastal marine fish that tolerate water of low salinities, just like the scat, *Scatophagus argus,* seen here with them. These two brackish water fishes are regularly imported from the Far East in commercial quantities.

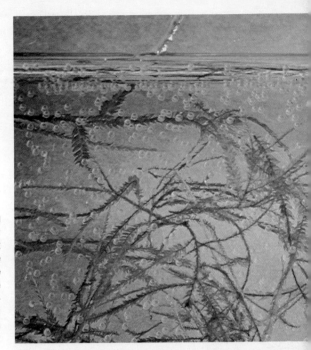

Aquarium spawning of *Monodactylus sebae* indicates that the eggs float to the surface, provided the water is saline. The eggs sink to the bottom when spawning occurs in fresh water.

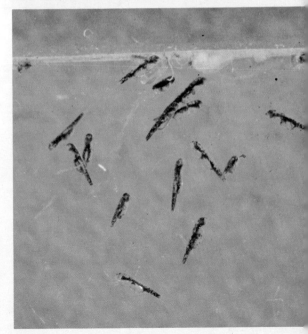

Failure to feed on food of the right size leads to gradual starvation and death of newly hatched *Monodactylus sebae* fry. Food size is thus the critical factor in the successful rearing of monos in captivity.

117

sumption of 1 gm of 6 cm fishes, and each gm of 15 cm fishes is allowed rather less oxygen than that of 6 cm fish. The base line is the 6 cm tropical fish, which is allowed 125 cm² of surface area—a generous allowance—and all estimates should be divided by 3 for cold-water fishes and by 6 for fancy goldfish varieties. The 125 cm² allowance is intended to permit further growth and good health. The fishes would not be expected to show distress if their numbers were doubled, but they would not flourish so well. The estimates are clearly approximate and could be misleading in special cases, but from experience it is felt that they are a much better guide than other current recommendations. It will be apparent to the thinking reader that fat fishes of the same length are likely to use more oxygen than slimmer fishes, but this fact is fortunately minimized by the greater activity and therefore greater oxygen need of the slimmer, minnow-like types. One major alteration in the rule applies to the anabantids, which, when the labyrinth is developed, require only half the surface area per fish otherwise recommended (the labyrinth is present in all but young fry).

| Body length of fish in cm * | No. of fishes per 1,000 cm² of surface area of tank | Square cm per fish |
|---|---|---|
| 1 | 400 | 2.5 |
| 2 | 110 | 9 |
| 3 | 50 | 20 |
| 4 | 25 | 40 |
| 5 | 12 | 80 |
| 6 | 8 | 125 |
| 8 | 5 | 200 |
| 10 | 2 | 500 |
| 12 | 1 | 750 |
| 15 | 1 | 1100 |

* The body length *excludes* the tail fin.

*Example 1*: In a 60-liter tank with a surface area of 1800 cm², the following fishes are held. Are they likely to be overcrowded, or can even more be added?

8 characins, each about 4 cm long    6 barbs, each about 6 cm long
12 characins, each about 5 cm long    6 gouramis, each about 6 cm long
4 barbs, each about 5 cm long    2 cichlids, each about 8 cm long

We calculate:

| | | |
|---|---|---|
| 8 fishes at 4 cm need 8 x 40 cm² | = | 320 cm² |
| 16 fishes at 5 cm need 16 x 80 cm² | = | 1280 cm² |
| 6 fishes at 6 cm need 6 x 62.5 cm² | = | 750 cm² |
| 2 fishes at 8 cm need 2 x 200 cm² | = | 400 cm² |
| Total | | 3125 cm² |

*Conclusion*: The fishes are crowded and cannot be expected to thrive. Certainly no more should be added, and it would be best to omit a few or to add aeration.

*Example 2*: What size of tank should be used to house 100 fry of average length 1 cm, with room to grow them to 2 cm before moving them again?

It is the final size of the fry that matters, hence the tank should have a surface area of 100 x 9 cm². If they were to reach an average of 3 cm in length, then 100 x 20 cm² or 2,000 cm² would be needed—i.e., a 60- to 80-liter tank. Note that small fry cannot stand too brisk aeration, although one or more moderate trickles would be very useful.

## MODIFYING FACTORS

The addition of plants to the aquarium does not much affect the calculations above. If the fishes are not unduly crowded, then additional daylight help from plants is unnecessary but no disadvantage, and their nighttime absorption of oxygen will not much matter, particularly as the fishes are inactive and so consume less oxygen and produce less carbon dioxide themselves. If the tank is crowded, the daytime activity of the plants makes all the difference, but at night, despite the fishes' quietude, the added burden of plant respiration is likely to make conditions very hard. This may be observed in many a crowded and heavily planted tank; while daylight lasts or artificial illumination is supplied, the fishes are quite comfortable, but at night, and very soon after they have been plunged into darkness, they are gasping at the surface. They may and usually do survive this treatment, but the nighttime stress should be relieved by aeration or, better still, by lowering the fish population of the tank. There is good reason to believe that the accumulation of an excess of carbon dioxide is more important in most circumstances than is lack of oxygen and that the dark, overcrowded tank is suffering more because the plants are failing to remove carbon dioxide than because they are failing to produce oxygen. Aeration helps because some of the carbon dioxide is "blown off" by the water movement.

From the above, it will be clear that the best solution for in-

A female guppy giving birth to her young. The thin membrane breaks open immediately and the fry starts to swim freely.

A female guppy and one of the fry from an earlier brood. The obviously enlarged abdomen of this guppy indicates the certainty of a forthcoming batch of young soon.

A pair of wild swordtails, *Xiphophorus helleri*, from Honduras, Central America. The green variety of domestic swordtail represents the wild form in the hobby.

Note the much shorter sword and the absence of a distinct color pattern in this marigold strain of fancy swordtail.

creasing fish capacity is water movement, usually supplied by aeration. This can double the safety margin, so that the fish population may be doubled in a well-aerated tank, but *only* if the tank is also well-planted and clean or if the water is partly changed frequently to eliminate waste material. Water movement tends to stir up waste material and aid its more rapid solution in the water, and adequate provision for purification is needed. A filter does not necessarily fulfill these requirements, as it may act as a very efficient dissolving plant for the waste products and help to poison the water even though it keeps it clear.

Only if the filter is provided with absorbent or adsorbent material such as activated carbon or one of the new chemical absorbents is it likely to do other than remove gross particulate material, unless it is also a biological filter.

One of the factors that definitely tends to reduce fish capacity is the presence of waste materials, especially unconsumed food or dead plant material, less so actual excretory products of the fishes. All these substances use oxygen and produce carbon dioxide while rotting and thus reduce the safety margin for the fishes. Another factor is the presence of invertebrate animal life other than air-breathers. Colonial sponges or polyps or an excess of unconsumed living worms or crustaceans may make conditions dangerous for fishes.

A final important factor is temperature. Oxygen dissolves more readily in cooler water, so that at 10 °C a liter of water can hold about 7.7 ml of oxygen (or the oxygen from about 150 ml of air) whereas at 27 °C it holds only 5.6 ml. This, by the way, is the maximum oxygen capacity, assuming pure water without the inevitable presence of carbon dioxide and other gases which replace some of the oxygen in ordinary circumstances. Thus, in the average tank, a content of around 3 ml per liter is quite good and adequate for the fishes; some can take down to about 1.5 ml without severe distress. When the temperature rises the fishes become considerably more active and their rate of consumption of oxygen also rises, both because of this and for more fundamental chemical reasons, with the net result that the fish capacity of the tank falls quite rapidly with increased temperature. In tropical tanks, which do not usually experience a wide temperature variation, this is not likely to matter much, but in a

122

cold-water tank which undergoes a considerable rise, as on a hotter day than usual, serious results may occur. As far as is known, fishes resemble other cold-blooded animals in that their metabolic rate (the rate, among other things, of oxygen consumption) is about doubled for every 10 °C rise, so that a rise from 15 °C to 25 °C can tax a crowded tank so much as to cause deaths.

The question of balance in a fish tank is therefore a relative affair and not as pictured by the average aquarist. The greatest "adjusters" are the fishes themselves, which can vary their respiratory rate about tenfold and thus cope with a wide range of oxygen availability or carbon dioxide excess. This does not mean, however, that they can live in a tenth of the normal oxygen concentration, as the rate at which the gills can take it from the water falls sharply with a decrease in concentration, so that the average fish is in distress when a 50% fall occurs. That is why some fishes, particularly those used to running water or the open sea, cannot stand ordinary aquarium life, as the oxygen content even at best is below their tolerance.

## WATER QUALITY

Water from the faucet may be perfectly satisfactory for the aquarium immediately as it is drawn, but often it is not. It is likely to contain free chlorine, especially in city areas, and it is possibly under sufficient pressure to contain an excess of other dissolved gases, although a poisonous excess of oxygen, sometimes claimed to be a danger, seems unlikely. It may be of the wrong salinity or hardness, and it may be too acid or too alkaline. However, in most districts tap water is perfectly satisfactory after standing for a day or two, a process sometimes called "conditioning." This allows for gas exchange between the water and the air, which may be hastened by aeration or by boiling and cooling again, but dangerous pH changes may follow the latter.

Chlorinated water may be rendered immediately safe by the addition of 10 mg of sodium thiosulphate (the "hypo" of photographers) per liter of water, as far as its chlorine content is concerned, not water treated with other new chlorinated compounds. Distilled water or even filtered snow may be used; if so, salts should be added, as such water is too "pure" and will not

Most probably one of the platies, *Xiphophorus maculatus,* you will find in a pet shop will be of the red variety. This strain is already genetically fixed, and you can expect uniform progeny if they are properly bred.

**Opposite:** Two color varieties of mollies, *Poecilia sphenops,* with lyretails: marbled (top) and black (bottom). This black variety has an unusually deep body and a long dorsal fin.

support life adequately. Suitable salts are:

    3 teaspoons (20 gm) of common salt
    1 teaspoon (7 gm) of magnesium sulphate
    1 teaspoon (7 gm) of potassium sulphate
    per 100 liters of distilled or snow water.

These salts are, however, *not* required when it is desired to breed certain fishes, or even for the maintenance of many species, as long as they are not suddenly moved from a salty tank to a purer one.

Rain water may need similar treatment, but it is dangerous to use in towns, for on the way down it collects a lot of dirt and harmful chemicals from the air and may be very toxic. Snow is less liable to be so polluted, even in towns.

Hard water contains dissolved salts absent, or relatively so, from soft water. Very soft water may have salts added as for distilled water, whereas normally hard water doesn't need them. For orientation purposes, here are typical analyses of sea water, hard water, and soft water, in percentages of various important salts:

|  | Sodium chloride | Potassium sulphate | Magnesium sulphate | Calcium carbonate, etc. | Total |
|---|---|---|---|---|---|
| Sea water | 2.8 | 0.14 | 0.66 | 0.10 | 3.7 |
| Hard water | 0.005 | 0.007 | 0.007 | 0.015 | 0.034 |
| Soft water | 0.004 | 0.000 | 0.000 | 0.002 | 0.006 |

Aquarium water can with advantage contain rather more salts (but not more calcium) than typical hard water (except for special purposes, such as the breeding of neon tetras), and up to 0.1% of total solids is quite in order. Most fish can take much more.

Hard water is usually alkaline; soft water is usually neutral to acid in reaction. Acidity and alkalinity are measured on a scale which goes from 0 to 14, called the pH scale. Neutral water has a pH of 7, acid water has a pH of less than 7. Strong acids are down in the 1 to 2 region, strong alkalis up in the 12 to 13 region. A weak acid like carbonic acid (dissolved carbon dioxide) even at full strength has a pH of only about 4, a weak alkali like sodium bicarbonate a pH of about 9, and this is approximately the range seen in natural waters. Few fishes can stand this entire range, but most can be happy anywhere between 6 and 8, and many do not show distress when well beyond these limits. Most aquarium plants flourish best at a slightly alkaline pH.

In community tanks, a pH around neutral is desirable, but in specialist tanks a pH more suited to the particular fishes being kept should be maintained. The tetras prefer an acid pH, for example, and so do angelfish and many other South American fishes from soft, acid waters. Barbs, on the other hand, and many cichlids are more indifferent to their surroundings, but some of the cichlids from Africa live in highly alkaline waters and must be kept at a pH of 8.6 to 9.2, typical of Lake Tanganyika. Brackish water fishes such as *Scatophagus* or *Selenotoca* species need hard, alkaline water around pH 8.0 to thrive. When breeding, a more critical pH is often needed, so that a tetra which can live, even if not optimally, at pH 7.2, may need a pH of 6.0 or less to produce viable eggs.

The pH of a tank is not usually constant and tends to rise during the day, as carbonic acid gas is removed by the plants, and to fall at night, when both plants and animals produce it. The extent to which this affects pH readings depends on the degree of aeration, the atmosphere in the room, and the fish and plant density. In a crowded tank in a room with rather foul air, such as an exhibition tank at a crowded indoor show, the pH may fall alarmingly in a few hours to values of 5.5 or lower.

## MEASURING AND ADJUSTING pH

Measuring pH is, perhaps, the most commonly done test already. It involves only a determination of acidity or alkalinity with a suitable indicator or, less accurately, papers impregnated with indicator to be dipped into the tank. A suitable measure of pH is given by adding to 10 ml of tank water (about 2 teaspoons) ½ ml of indicator solution (about 10 drops) containing 0.1% bromthymol blue. The resultant color may be compared with a chart or other color comparator provided by dealers, and it changes from yellow when acid, through green when near neutral, to blue when alkaline, over a range of pH 6.0 (acid) to 7.6 (alkaline). Most of us get so familiar with the look of bromthymol blue that we can guess the pH pretty accurately.

Adjusting pH is best done with acid and alkaline sodium phosphates, or on the alkaline side alone with sodium bicarbonate. A suitable mixture of phosphates, however, gives a *buffered* solution

A display community tank can be installed to appear as part of any room's decor. However, the equipment must be inspected and maintained regularly or you run the risk of water overflowing and damaging valuable items near the aquarium. For safety, such items are best placed elsewhere.

which is so-called because it resists change in pH for as long as the chemicals in it remain intact. Unfortunately, this may be only a few days in an aquarium. Acid sodium phosphate ($NaH_2PO_4$) has a pH in solution of about 4, whereas alkaline sodium phosphate ($Na_2HPO_4$) has a pH of about 9.5. An equal mixture of the two gives pH 6.8, which is almost neutral (pH 7.0).

To adjust the pH of a body of water, obtain 1% solutions of the two phosphates. Then take one liter of water from the tank and *slowly* add small quantities of whichever phosphate is needed, testing at intervals until the correct pH is obtained. Then, having measured the amount required to bring a liter of water to the correct pH, multiply by the number of liters in the aquarium and add slowly to the water. Remember that the pH of a tank should not be changed too much at one time if fish are present; steps of about 0.3 are enough.

When the tank is at the desired pH, a buffered mixture can be added by reading from the accompanying table the quantities of $NaH_2PO_4$ and $Na_2HPO_4$ which, when mixed together, give a buffer of the same acidity or alkalinity. About 10 ml (2 teaspoons) of this mixture of 1% solutions per gallon may then be added to the aquarium. The pH of a tank should be adjusted *after* making all other adjustments needed.

| Parts of 1% $Na_2HPO_4$ | Parts of 1% $NaH_2PO_4$ | Resultant pH |
|---|---|---|
| 1 | 9 | 5.9 |
| 2 | 8 | 6.2 |
| 3 | 7 | 6.5 |
| 4 | 6 | 6.6 |
| 5 | 5 | 6.8 |
| 6 | 4 | 7.0 |
| 7 | 3 | 7.2 |
| 8 | 2 | 7.4 |
| 9 | 1 | 7.7 |

## MEASURING AND ADJUSTING HARDNESS

Measuring hardness, much less frequently practiced among aquarists, is becoming more essential as we try to keep and breed the rarer varieties. There are several types of outfit available

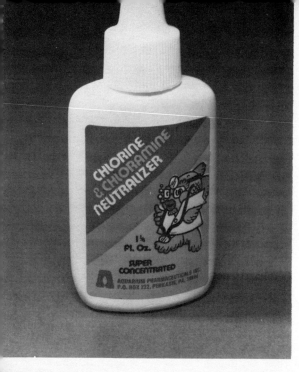

**Left:** Dechlorinating agents if needed are available. However, always read the directions carefully prior to using.
**Below:** Measuring the pH is made easy by a color indicator chart included in most pH kits.

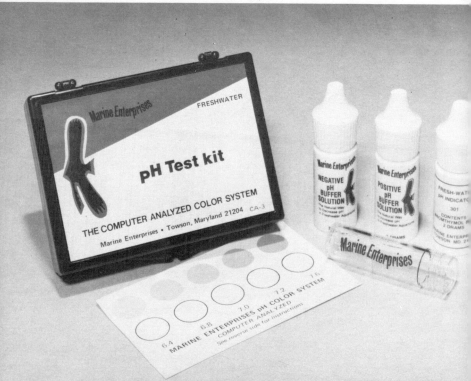

which may be obtained from your dealer, most of which seem to give a sufficiently accurate answer. A frequently preferred method is the "Versenate" method, as in the B.D.H. hardness testing kit. Hardness is usually expressed as parts per million (ppm) of calcium carbonate or as "degrees" of hardness in Germany. One German degree equals 18 parts per million. Magnesium, which may be present even in greater quantity than calcium, causes hardness and is measured in with the calcium as though it were that element. It may, if necessary, be separately measured in a modification of the Versenate method. Neither hardness nor pH have anything to do with salinity, the sodium chloride (common salt) content of the water.

Adjusting hardness may be essential for breeding some of the more difficult fishes, when the water may need either softening (as for characins) or hardening (as for some live-bearers). Water may be softened to a variable extent by boiling, but this is hardly practical in an established aquarium. If the water is not much too hard, it may be partially replaced by distilled water or clean rain water to an extent indicated by the degree of softening required. Finally, it may be softened to any extent required by the use of a water-softening pillow or a filter containing a suitable ion-exchange resin (water-softening pillows usually contain such resins but are fairly slow in action). The ion-exchange resins, which may be obtained commercially, are prepared in granular form and are usually intended for large-scale filters. When used for softening water they replace any other metals present, including calcium and magnesium which are responsible for hardness, by sodium or by hydrogen. The sodium form is best to use, since the small amount of sodium freed into the water rarely matters and may be preferable to the corresponding amount of (acid) hydrogen. If necessary, however, a combination of resins may be used to remove everything and give virtually distilled water. A resin such as Zeo-Karb 225 will soften one or two hundred liters per 100 gm of resin, which may then be re-activated by a simple chemical procedure.

Hardening water is very easy—simply add the required amount of calcium chloride to the tank. If your tank has a hardness of 70 parts per million (as calcium) and you want to have 200 ppm, then 130 ppm must be added. This is 130 mg calcium per liter.

# MEASURING AND ADJUSTING SALINITY

Measuring salinity in the freshwater tank is very rarely done, even by experts, yet it is both important and easy. The simplest way is probably to titrate against silver nitrate, using potassium chromate as an indicator. Marine water contains up to 3% sodium chloride, typical tap water only about 0.005%, or 50 ppm. Aquarium water often builds up a salt content of 500 ppm or more, particularly when salt is purposely added. Beyond 1000 ppm plants are likely to suffer—some do not like more than 300 or 400 ppm.

Adjusting salinity resembles adjustments for hardness. Water which is too salty may be diluted with pure water or "desalted" with ion-exchange resins. This is best done with the combination of resins mentioned above, either mixed in a single filter or kept separate, when each can be regenerated and used again.

It will more frequently be necessary to increase salinity, when any change is needed at all. This is easily done by adding the requisite amount of pure sodium chloride or butchers' salt (rock salt). Do not use table salt, which gives a cloudy solution because it contains other material to make it "run." Remember that one level teaspoon per 4 liters increases salinity by about 1000 ppm (0.1%), which is ample for most purposes.

If distilled water is used at the start, measurements of pH, etc., may be dispensed with and suitable chemicals added straight away. Thus, 40 liters of distilled water to which are added five level teaspoons of rock salt and 100 ml of an equal mixture of sodium phosphates will be of practically nil hardness, 500 ppm salinity and approx. pH 6.8.

Only after making measurements of pH, hardness and salinity do we know enough about the water in a tank, or water we propose to introduce into a tank, to use it intelligently. There are other measurements we could make, such as the amount of nitrogen or organic matter as an index of purity or the amounts of dissolved gases as an index of the capacity of the water to support life. These may be important on special occasions, but the measurement of pH, hardness and salinity is important on frequent occasions and is almost *always* needed for sustained success in breeding many species of fish.

The following table, taken from various sources, including the author's own tanks, gives some instances of the pH, hardness and salinity of various types of water:

| Type of water | pH | Hardness p.p.m. | Salinity p.p.m. |
|---|---|---|---|
| Hard tap water | 7.8 | 270 | 50 |
| Soft tap water | 6.7 | 65 | 52 |
| Very soft tap water | 6.5 | 12 | 47 |
| Rain water (clean) | 5.6 | 2 | 0 |
| Brackish creek | 7.4 | 780 | 2800 |
| Characin tank | 6.6 | 18 | 46 |
| Barb tank * | 6.6 | 72 | 470 |
| Goby tank * | 7.6 | 260 | 1270 |
| Community tank* | 6.9 | 93 | 285 |

Some salt or sea water had purposely been added to the starred tanks to make them suitable for the types of fish they hold. In the characin tank, very soft water had developed naturally from tap water originally containing 50 to 60 ppm of calcium carbonate.

## PEAT WATER

Some areas where aquarium fishes are found in the wild are characterized by so-called "brown" water or even "black" water, which is very darkly colored, like tea or even coffee when looked into from above. This water has soaking in it a great deal of humus, or old leaves and forest debris, and it is usually soft and acid. This is, in part, caused by the soaking, which tends to remove hardness and acidify the water. Such water suits most of the characins and many of the cyprinodonts, and quite a list of other fishes, too. It is usually unsuitable for live-bearers, although they may become used to it. It may be produced artificially by soaking soft water with peat or peat-moss, when the same brown color develops and the water becomes acid. It is best to boil the peat before using it and to discard the water used for this, as its action may otherwise be toxic or too extreme. If the brown color is objectionable, it may be removed by filtration with activated charcoal of a *very fine* preferably gas-absorbent grade.

Peat water is not particularly nice to look at, unless more or less decolorized as above, but a number of serious aquarists now keep their fishes in such water, usually with about a 1 cm layer of peat at the bottom. Plants may be anchored by glass weights if it is desired to have them present. The colors of fishes develop more fully in such water, although it may be more difficult to see them also! The real importance of the water is for breeding, which is strikingly improved in some varieties by the technique, but more about this will follow. In addition, a layer of peat absorbs a certain amount of waste material and affords protection for eggs which may be deposited in it. The particular properties of peat-soaked water are supposed to be the presence of certain "humic" acids and the softening effect of peat on water which is not too hard initially. Some authors believe that the water can be copied by adding small amounts of tannic acid and by softening the water with ion-exchange resins, but this is not certain.

If peat water is used, it may be prepared by having a large reservoir available in which tap water is softened by ion-exchange filtration (if necessary) and either filtered through a large volume of peat, 500 gm per 100 liters, or stirred around by aeration with peat at the bottom of the tank. If aliquots are taken for use at intervals and the reservoir is kept full, a gentle turnover is maintained and suitable water of not too dark a quality is obtained regularly.

## NEW AND OLD WATER

The earlier aquarists were great conservationists with their aquarium water. When they siphoned off detritus and mulm, they usually filtered it and returned as much as possible to the tank. As a result, the water gradually acquired a rich wine color and a limpid clarity. The latter is very attractive, and it is surprising how yellow or even reddish the water can become without causing comment, unless a sample is compared with fresh, colorless water, when the difference is very obvious. The same applies to a moderate degree to peat water.

This "aged" water was supposed to have become more suited to the fishes than fresher (although not necessarily completely new) water. The thesis was, and still is for that matter, that fishes make water in which they live more suitable for themselves and even poisonous to other species not present in the tank. There seems to be little foundation for this belief, and it is certain that the same water, kept long enough, becomes poisonous to all fishes, even in the presence of growing plants. Toxicity to other species may well be the result of their inability to take a sudden exposure to water to which the permanent inhabitants have become gradually accustomed, as it has become steadily charged with waste products. However, the question is not settled and would repay more study. It has even been suggested that some "animal protein" factor is involved, but this is again very conjectural. As water evaporates and is replaced without removal of some of the tank water itself, it also tends to become harder and harder. However, a soft tap water source may steadily become softer, as a certain amount of salts of calcium and magnesium is used in the growth of plants and fishes.

Both expectation and experience now concur in advising a steady change-over of tank water. This may not need to be very much; usually 5 to 10% per week or fortnight is ample, but in crowded, badly illuminated tanks a change of 20 to 30% per week may be a decided advantage. Even in winter, when the gas content of fresh tap water is highest, the danger of such a volume of replacement is negligible, but, if preferred, the water may be left to stand for a day or two before use. Of course, the new water must be at the right temperature; never rely on the heater to take care of sudden additions of cold water to a warm tank. Even if the fish escape immediate chilling in the cold stream, the overall temperature after mixing may have fallen dangerously.

The qualities implied by the term "old water" are often therefore not really age but suitability. It is water which does not contain noxious gases or solids, is at the right pH, has the right salinity and hardness, and has the right content of algae, infusoria, and perhaps bacteriophages. And the word "right" differs according to whether the water is intended for a community tank, for spawning a particular species, or for raising fry.

## CLOUDY WATER

Water may become cloudy for a number of reasons. *Green cloudiness* is due to the presence of green algae, usually brought on by too much light in the presence of organic materials in solution. It is fundamentally healthy water, but it spoils the appearance of a tank and is usually not desired, except for raising fry. If it becomes very thick, there is danger that the rapidly growing algae will suddenly die and foul the water. The first sign of this is a slight yellowing of the water, which then rapidly turns fetid and is very dangerous to the fishes. It should be entirely changed without delay, using fresh tap water at the right temperature rather than taking the risk of leaving the fishes as they are. A store of spare "aged" water is commonly kept by experienced aquarists for just such an emergency.

Cleanliness, moderate light, no crowding of tanks, and the presence of plenty of higher plants, especially floating plants, help to prevent the appearance of green cloudiness. Tanks relying wholly or predominantly on electric illumination practically never develop green water, mainly because they do not receive excessive illumination. Acidity of the water makes for cleanliness, but not for good plant growth, so that both the algae and the higher plants are discouraged together. It is often said that a partial or nearly complete change of water only serves to stimulate further algal growth; however, this does not always occur, and green water may be cured immediately by siphoning it off—plus any debris in the tank—and replacing it with fresh, conditioned water.

*Gray cloudiness* may be due to infusoria, bacteria, fungi, or just dirt. It often follows the setting up of a tank, sometimes because the gravel was not washed thoroughly, but often because there is a burst of animal life which starts ahead of the algae. This cloudiness, whether dirt or infusoria, usually disappears in a few days and is not dangerous. Bacterial or fungal cloudiness is a bad sign, usually seen in established tanks which are "going bad." It may be caused by excessive decaying matter, usually dry food but sometimes a dead fish or mollusk, by insufficient light, by overcrowding, or by the use of unsuitable gravel or rock, which may provide niches and crannies where excreta and food are caught and decay. Although attention must be paid to the basic causes, such as overcrowding, gray cloudiness may often be temporarily corrected by brisk aeration or by the addition of disinfectants and antibiotics. Another effective method with both gray and green cloudiness is to place one or two large freshwater mussels in the tank for a few days. These will clear water when an ordinary filter may not, although one using diatomaceous earth as a filter capsule will usually do so. Chemicals which cause clumping of fine material in the water are also available, and it is then taken out by an ordinary filter.

## REMOVAL OF MULM

In the course of replacing some of the water at intervals of one or two weeks as recommended, it is easy to siphon off much of the mulm from the bottom of the tank. A convenient way to do this is to take a glass tube of ½ to 1 cm in diameter and slightly shorter than the aquarium depth if it is left straight or a little longer if the top is given an angle bend to prevent the rubber tubing which is attached to the glass tube from kinking. The business end of the glass tube should be softened by heat and then gently pressed onto a flat surface, holding the tube upright, so that the entrance is slightly constricted, to prevent pebbles, snails, and so forth, from getting into the tube and clogging it up. Any that do enter will be small enough to pass readily through the siphon. The rubber tubing should reach for up to 1 meter outside the tank below the water level, so as to give a convenient head of pressure.

The siphon is started by sucking the end of the rubber tubing with the glass tube immersed, or, if preferred, by filling it with water by dipping in the tank. With a little practice, it is possible to start the siphon without getting a mouth full of water. Self-starting siphons are also now available. The rate of flow is controlled by pinching the rubber tubing, and the siphon is then run gently over the aquarium bottom like a vacuum cleaner. The end of the glass tube may also be poked well into the sand, sucking up sample "bores" to see if all is well and to see that underneath the surface the sand is not becoming foul and gray with bacteria. If it is, it is wise to go on siphoning the gravel away until the foul patch is removed and to replace it with fresh gravel afterwards. With experience, it is possible to remove three-quarters of the bottom of a tank, leaving the plants undisturbed, and replace it by running clean *dry* gravel down a funnel under the surface of the water. If the gravel is wet, it sticks and must be washed into the tank, which of course may be done, or it may be put in by hand and the plants afterwards well shaken to remove sand grains. The foul gravel may be washed and dried off and left in the sun or in a bleaching solution such as is used for washing clothes, and used again.

The base of the siphon may be flared out like a small funnel, which, if plunged into the gravel, does not lift much or even any of the actual gravel but draws out other matter and helps considerably in preventing the major operation just described. However, a well set-up tank does not often develop serious gravel trouble in any case.

There are a number of aquarium gadgets on the market for the mechanical removal of mulm and other materials. The most popular is the filter, dealt with in detail later, but there are also little "vacuum cleaners" available for use with an air pump instead of the single siphon just described. They may be very efficient in clearing the mulm and clarifying the water, but their use does not involve the removal of some of the water, which should be done even though little or no visible mulm remains to be siphoned off.

## REMOVAL OF FIXED ALGAE

Green algae will cause not only green water, but filamentous forms will coat the inside of the glass if there is too much light. These algae may be removed with a scraper, essentially a razor blade on a convenient handle, or, more easily, with steel wool or plastic. Wrap a small ball of steel wool around the end of a stick and rub the glass with moderate pressure. It usually takes only a couple of minutes to clean a large tank thoroughly. When removing algae at the base of the tank, be careful not to get gravel caught in the steel wool, as it may scratch the glass badly.

Under electric illumination, blue-green algae are more likely to be a nuisance, settling not only on the glass, but also on the plants. These may be scraped from the glass as usual, but to remove them from the plants is almost impossible. Cut down the light and hope that it disappears, or remove all fishes, snails, etc., and treat with 5 parts per million copper sulphate (crystalline) for a few hours, afterwards removing nearly all the water and refilling before introducing fishes again.

ALGAE
SCRAPER
DUAL CLEANING HEAD

The marketplace has no lack of cleaning devices designed for the aquarium. Some examples are magnetic type (left) and dual type (right) algae scrapers and a whole array of brushes (below) for cleaning the tank and its equipment.

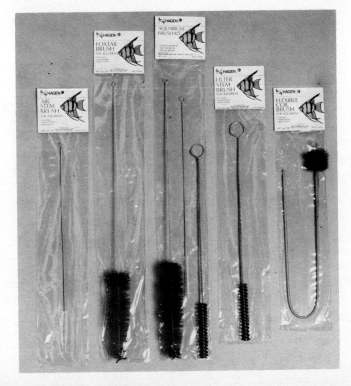

# ROUTINE CHECKS

The aquarist gets to know the look of a healthy tank, but even after much experience he may miss the early signs of trouble if he doesn't look carefully for specific symptoms. He must learn to look at the component parts of the set-up and to notice anything that may spell trouble so that corrective action may be taken at an effective stage. Points to remember are:

The *smell* of a healthy tank is earthy and pleasant. Look for the cause of any departure from this.

The *plants* should be of good color and not decaying in part or whole. Remove any large decaying leaves, stems or roots and test the pH if decay continues.

The *water* should of course be clear or mildly green, and its surface should be clean and without a film of dust, oily material or bacteria.

The *gravel* should be clean, loose, and not gray below the surface. If it is disturbed, no bubbles should rise from it.

The *fishes* should look alert and well, with fins clear and held away from the body. "Clamped" fins or peculiar swimming motions mean impending trouble. The fishes should have no blemishes or strings of excreta hanging from them.

The *corners* of the tank and hidden crannies should be searched for dead fish or sick fish hiding away.

The *temperature* should be checked as a daily routine in tropical tanks.

# CHAPTER FIVE

## Setting Up a Tank

The first important consideration when starting an aquarium is its location. Daylight is not essential, and it may be maintained in perfect health with electric illumination alone. Indeed, the control of plant growth, both in extent and direction, and the suppression of green water or other unwanted algae is much easier with artificial light. Details are dealt with later, but in general a tank should have at least 8 to 10 hours of illumination a day (12 to 14 hours is not too long) and should not receive more than about 2 hours of direct natural sunlight, less with a small tank in summer, which may otherwise seriously overheat. Drafty locations must be avoided, and so must the tops of radiators, which heat the gravel and cause the plants to wilt and can overheat the tank far too easily. Thus, the popular window location over a radiator is not to be recommended.

### SAND OR GRAVEL

The purpose of the gravel is to hold down rooted plants and to provide decoration. If too fine, gravel packs tightly and prevents the roots from penetrating; it also promotes the growth of anaerobic bacteria—those that thrive in oxygen-free surroundings and turn the sand gray or black. If it is too coarse, the plants get little grip and work free, and unconsumed food and other detritus get down into it and are not easily removed. There are many varieties of artificial compost now available, with selected grain sizes and colors. Which may be preferred depends on taste and on whether an undergravel filter is to be used. This is discussed below.

Coarse river gravel, preferably with a variable grain size for pleasant appearance, is perhaps the best. It should be deep enough to provide adequate root space for the plants used, which will vary from 2.5 to 7.5 cm. In all but the smallest tanks, 5 cm at the back and less in front is about right, but it may be banked up much more than this if desired for decorative effects. However, a great depth tends sooner or later to become foul, and it is best to avoid it or to pack the deeper areas with rock beneath the gravel.

The placing of deep gravel at the back automatically provides for three things. First, it looks pleasant, giving the aquarium base a gentle forward slope which best exhibits the content. Second, it provides for the largest plants to be sited at the back, where they are usually required. Third, it encourages the mulm to collect toward the front of the tank, whence it is easily removed.

Before use, gravel must be thoroughly washed. Even if supplied as "washed," it will normally require some further washing. Really dirty material may need 20 or 30 swirlings in fresh buckets of water or half an hour's thorough hosing in a shallow container. Failure to do this may cause cloudy water for weeks or more serious trouble.

European aquarists frequently use peat, loam, or earth beneath the gravel or in pockets of rock to nourish the plants. The experience of most of us is that such materials sooner or later cause trouble; either they get stirred up and make a sorry mess of the water or they turn bad and have to be removed. Nevertheless, their use is clearly practicable with care, and it is said that the plant growth in aquaria so planted is outstanding. This growth is naturally a result of organic materials supplied beneath the gravel, and the plants may not, therefore, be performing their essential function of removing much of the waste products of the fishes as well as they otherwise would. This is another of the points which have not been clarified, and further research and observation are needed before we can dismiss the use of these materials as undesirable. It may depend on whether an under-gravel filter is used.

## STONES, ROCKWORK, AND ORNAMENTS

These items are almost purely a matter of personal taste. There are occasions when stones are needed by the fishes, as in spawning some of the cichlids, but they have usually no essential function in other tanks except to look nice. Judges in shows have various theories about the relationship between stones and the gravel they lie in and about the direction of rock strata. Such considerations seem of importance only when specialist tanks simulating particular environments are in question.

It must be recalled that large rocks take up water volume, but the tank would have to be extraordinarily full of them before this would be likely to matter except when judging the amount of chemicals to add in the treatment of disease.

Ornaments such as treasure chests, divers, sea shells, and mermaids are liked by some aquarists and hated by others. As long as they are made of inert materials and are harmless to the fishes and water conditions, follow your own dictates. Sea shells or shell grit (sometimes used instead of gravel) are all right in the marine tank but will make the freshwater tank too alkaline.

## PLANTING

Select young, healthy-looking plants for setting up a tank, and, unless they come from an impeccable source, disinfect them or quarantine them. If you wish to use them immediately, a rapid wash in salt water (3 teaspoons per liter) or sea water of not more than 15 seconds' duration followed by a thorough wash in fresh water will be a good insurance. If you can wait, leave them for a couple of days in a solution of potassium permanganate at a strength of 3 mg per liter (3 parts per million) or use 8 mg per liter and leave for only 15 minutes. The longer period at lower strength is better.

Make a diagram of the desired scheme before going about the job, or it may turn out very different from that hoped for by the inexperienced. The higher-growing and larger plants look best at the back and sides, particularly the long, grass-like plants and the long-stemmed plants like *Cabomba*, *Myriophyllum*, and *Anacharis*. Then, perhaps in relationship to rocks or stones, may come groups of other plants, such as *Cryptocoryne*, *Echinodorus* or *Ludwigia*. These are best placed in groups of one type, not mixed up indiscriminately. In front, some of the smaller grasses or dwarf varieties of other plants may be used, but it is customary to leave a free swimming space in the center front. A particularly fine plant, such as an *Echinodorus*, is often used as a centerpiece in the larger tanks.

Then place about 4 cm of level gravel in the tank and smooth it

143

back and to the sides in the desired formation, placing any rocks and stones in position at this stage. Now place a large cup or jar in the front of the tank and gently pour water into it so that it gently overflows and fills the tank for a depth of 15 to 20 cm. This is a convenient depth for planting. Meanwhile keep the plants wet, as a short period of drying may kill or set them back severely. Cut back the roots of all plants to a length of 2.5 to 5 cm according to size, and anchor them by pushing them into the gravel about 2.5 cm forward of their eventual site and dragging them back or sideways through the gravel into position. This makes a slight mess of the arrangements, but it is easier than trying to push them into place in the usual way with sticks or tongs. It is superfluous to worry about spreading the roots nicely, as they decay and are replaced by new growth in most cases.

Plants that have a crown above the roots, like the grasses and *Cryptocoryne*, must be carefully planted so as to leave this crown exposed or they may wither and die. Others may be thrust into the gravel with less care, but it is best not to submerge too much stem and leaves as these may, in subsequently decaying, foul the tank. Leave small spaces between adjacent plants, about 1 to 2 cm at least with the grasses and tall, thin plants, and much more with bushy plants. Allowing for subsequent filling-out by growth and the striking of new plants, a typical 60-liter tank, with a floor area of 1800 cm², will need about three dozen back and side plants and a dozen central plants.

Planting sticks—long sticks with a notch in one end and perhaps a sharp, chisel-like blade at the other end—are useful for making additions when the rest of the plants are in place and for resetting plants that have floated up before becoming firmly rooted.

Planting trays are sometimes used. These are flat trays, usually of such dimensions that two or three of them fill the base of the tank. They are an advantage when it is required to empty the tank frequently, as for exhibition or breeding purposes, but require careful camouflage if they are not to be too obvious. Smaller trays may be used with advantage if set unobtrusively in the gravel or behind rocks and may house prize plants or varieties that need particular care or are moved from time to time to different tanks. It is best to use trays made of plastic, china, or earthenware, not of metal, however well coated, except with enamel.

When planting is complete, the tank may be filled. If the recommended 15 to 20 cm of water is already present and the tank is new, leave it for a day and then complete the filling, just in case of leaks. It is best *not* to fill a new tank and then empty it again before planting to clean it or to "test" for leaks, although modern all-glass tanks are usually safe.

Filling after planting must be done gently, so as not to disturb the gravel. Continue to pour into a jar up to 25 to 30 cm, but if the tank is deeper than this the rest can be poured in from 10 to 20 cm above the water level as long as the inflowing water creates a mass of bubbles, which break its force and prevent it from sweeping down onto the bottom. Fill to about 2 cm from the top —usually the tank looks best if the water-line is just hidden under the top of the frame, if there is one.

## HEATING AND LIGHTING

These subjects have a chapter to themselves, but a few general words are not out of place here. A tropical tank is usually heated electrically, with a control known as a thermostat which is set to keep the tank at about the same temperature all the time. Of course, the thermostat works only downward, and if the outside temperature rises above that set by the thermostat it cannot prevent the tank from getting warmer too. Actually, even fairly small tanks take quite a time to absorb heat from the air and do not usually heat up unduly as long as the night brings some relief.

Thermostat-heater combinations housed in a single tube are commonly used. However, a heavy-duty thermostat which clips onto the outside of a tank can be used to control several tanks—up to perhaps 10 or 15. When this is done, the tanks must be very similar in size and location or control of the temperature will not be achieved; otherwise, the rather sophisticated methods outlined in the next chapter may be employed. Most fishes are stimulated by small temperature swings, so that variations of a few degrees from time to time should cause no alarm, as long as there is no reason to think that anything is wrong with controls. Beware, however, of allowing the water level to fall very much without topping up, which easily occurs in large tanks. If the thermostat becomes appreciably exposed to air and not water, it will begin measuring the air temperature and in cold weather it may remain closed and cook the fishes.

Every independently heated tank should have a thermometer. There are various types, some floating and some fixed, and most of them are likely to be as much as 2 °C off either way. They should be carefully checked at, say, 20° and 30 °C against a standard mercury thermometer. A great advantage of the clock-type thermometer is that it can be fastened to the front glass of batteries of tanks so that the pointer is upright at the desired temperature and any departure of 1 °C or more from this is immediately apparent.

There is often a considerable top-to-bottom temperature difference in static tropical tanks. This is no cause for worry, as it mimics conditions in nature, where the heat of the sun frequently raises the temperature of the top water well above that of the lower strata and the fishes just stay down to keep cool.

Lighting other than daylight is supplied from the top. Side lighting sometimes gives interesting effects, but it causes many fishes to swim lopsidedly and may eventually upset them. Also the plants will grow towards the light and may look very odd when obliquely illuminated for any length of time. Lighting is now nearly always by fluorescent strips, but spotlights may be used for special effects or to encourage a particular plant to grow. A variety of types of tubes is now available, some specially designed to encourage plant growth and/or to bring out the colors of the fishes. Although expensive to install, fluorescent lighting is cheap to run and does not overheat the tank as did the older incandescent globes. In general, "daylight" or "warm white" fluorescents are best, perhaps combined in a large tank with a special plant growth tube which adds a soft, purplish light that both helps plants and looks attractive. Above and around the fluorescent tube is placed a hood with a reflector.

## COVERS

In addition to the cover afforded by a reflector, the top of the aquarium is best completely enclosed in some fashion. Glass is popular and necessary when light must enter through the cover.

Covers serve a number of purposes. They prevent fishes from

jumping out, and they prevent other creatures, from beetles to cats, from getting in. They also help to keep the tank warmer and prevent rapid evaporation. A tight-fitting cover, by the way, enclosing about 2 cm of air space, does not suffocate the fishes, which obtain plenty of oxygen from the air enclosed, even if the cover is really airtight (which it usually isn't). The removal of the cover or part of it one or more times per day for feeding is enough. A cover is best made in two pieces, so that either a strip along the front or a corner-piece can be lifted for feeding, etc. without removing the whole cover.

## INTRODUCING FISHES

When a tank has been set up, it is best left for several days before fishes are placed in it. During this period there is a chance to check that all is well, that no leaks have started, and that the temperature control of a tropical tank is satisfactory. Nothing is more disheartening than to set up a tank and place the fishes in it and then have to dismantle everything hurriedly and find an emergency home for them. This rest period also allows the plants to become settled and to start functioning, which they will do fully only after a week or two; more important, it allows some of the most troublesome fish diseases or parasites to die off, which they may do if they have been introduced by accident to the tank and no hosts are present. This is particularly important with the parasite known as "white spot," which does not live long without the presence of fishes and which is one of the most widespread of all fish troubles.

Look over all the fishes carefully before placing them in the tank, and if they seem all right there is no reason why they should not all be put into the new tank together, taking especial care not to chill them or to subject them to much of a pH change. The best way to avoid this is to float the plastic bags in which they have probably arrived in the water of the tank until the waters are at about the same temperature and then gradually mix the waters together. Do not overstock the tank; it is much better to understock it for the first few weeks. Once the tank has a fish population, do not introduce new fishes without a quarantine period, unless you *know* that they have been in a disease-free tank for at least two weeks and *know* that they have not been chilled on their way to you or subjected to any other risks. If they have traveled for more than a few hours, you can hardly be sure of this. Otherwise, they should be given two weeks' quarantine in a special tank, even if they look perfectly well. It is impossible for the owner of only a single community tank to do this, but at least he should well realize that he takes a risk every time he introduces strangers to the tank and he may think twice about placing any fishes there which are in any way subject to suspicion. The same applies to new plants. The new fishes can be floated in the main tank in a jar or bowl, but if this is done care must be taken to see that they are given enough room and air surface and that they don't jump into the tank.

If you have no spare isolation tank and have precious specimens in a tank to which you have decided to introduce new fishes, probably the best thing to do is absolutely nothing, except to keep a very watchful eye on all the inhabitants for several weeks and be ready to give immediate treatment for any recognizable malady and general treatment for any of the ills of unknown origin or specific treatment.

If a new fish does develop disease, don't always blame the previous owner or the dealer. Disease *may* be present in your tank and the new fish *may* have caught it from your own stock, which may not be showing it actively. Or the new fish may have been weakened in transit and fall sick after its arrival. Subsequently, the whole tank may be affected, as it is quite common for a latent disease to start on a new rampage once it has been given a fillip by the presence of a susceptible host. From this host it can spread back to the rest in heightened form. This is seen commonly with white spot and fungus.

**CATCHING FISHES**

Nets for the purpose of catching adult fishes in small tanks should be as large as possible and not very deep. They should preferably not come to a point anywhere, either like a dunce's cap or with pointed corners, but should be gently rounded so as to give minimum risk of injury to the fishes. They may be made of mosquito netting or other suitable fabric, with reasonably wide pores so as to offer small resistance to the water. Plastic nets are popular, but be wary of harsh fabrics which can damage fishes.

Nets for catching fry should be quite shallow so that they do not cause the fry to "ball up" at all, but when in use they must be carefully watched, as fry usually jump. Fry may also be siphoned off, although even when very small they are often remarkably adept at dodging.

Most fishes can be caught without much fuss if you are not in a hurry, but once the necessary iron self-control is lost a tank is easily wrecked. It is a good idea to try stealth first—gently approach the fish with a good-sized net and try to slip it under the fish and lift it cleanly out without causing any panic. If this or your patience fails, you may chase more actively, usually with little success. When this stage is reached, it is best to stop and try again in a few minutes; but if you are in a great hurry, then place the net at one end, well ballooned out into the darkest part of the tank, and chase the fishes into it with a free hand or another net. Then, unless you want to remove the lot, lift the net and rest it on the frame of the tank with the fishes in water but still trapped. Finally, remove the specimens wanted with a small tumbler or cup. Do not handle small fishes if you can avoid it. Large fishes, including goldfishes, are often best caught and removed gently by hand, if possible, as they struggle in a net and may injure themselves more that way than if gently handled.

Fishes can often be tricked by a white net with a dark patch at the center. They take this to be a hole in the net and rush towards it.

The best daylight maneuver has been left until last. If your fishes have the common habit of all rushing to the top of the tank to be fed, they may often be caught practically all together with a single well-directed sweep of the net. If this misses, it is not usually so easy to repeat it with any success on the same occasion, so try later.

The best method of all, however, is to wait until the tank has been in darkness for at least half an hour. Switch the lights on and be ready to catch up any desired fishes within the next half minute. Almost all species remain motionless for this period and can be easily removed.

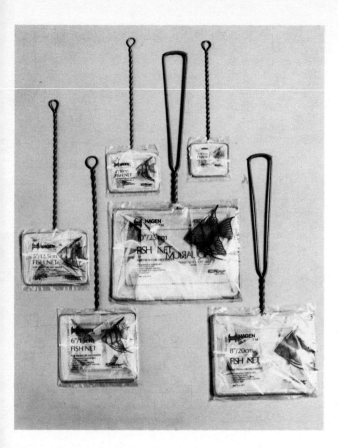

Choose a well-constructed net of a flexible, strong and mildew-resistant material and with a sturdy and rust-proof frame and handle.

Finally, do not move any fishes more than is absolutely necessary, particularly when they have been established in one tank for a long time. Sometimes a transfer to an apparently perfectly suitable tank with waters from the same source is fatal. This does not mean that most fishes cannot be safely moved—they can—but don't do it unnecessarily. Remember also that it is quite difficult to catch a fish without doing it some slight injury, and that all such abrasions may become the site of infection which may spread not only on the individual but throughout a whole tank or battery.

It should be noted that the above relates only to fresh-water aquaria. Marine tanks need special setting-up procedures not described here.

# CHAPTER SIX

## Lighting and Heating

Indoor aquaria that are not in a special fish room, rarely receive ideal illumination, which is natural daylight coming from directly overhead. If they get sufficient daylight, they usually receive it at an acute angle through a window at one side or at the back. This is satisfactory for most fishes and does not cause too much disturbance to plant growth as long as the tank doesn't get a great preponderance of very oblique light. If it does, the eventual result will be plants all growing at an angle or at least with leaves unevenly developed and fishes swimming at an angle, particularly the barbs and some of the characins, which seem to be very sensitive to lighting.

Much of this trouble can be rectified by a combination of shading and a mirror so directed that oblique light is reflected downwards into the tank more or less vertically. Of course, time of day and season of the year will need different adjustments for exact vertical illumination, but a surprising amount can be achieved with a fixed system which is adjusted only every few weeks.

Large tanks can stand quite a bit of direct sunlight, and, if it can be arranged so that this falls more on the back and sides and not much on the front glass, the former will become coated with a lush growth of algae, and the latter can be kept clear with only an occasional wiping with steel wool. The algae will act as automatic light screens and usually provide a very pleasant-looking background to the other plants, giving a look of maturity and depth to the tank and providing food for the fishes. Care must be taken to avoid overheating the tank, and it must be recalled that the tank goes on absorbing heat even when the algal coat has formed. A heat-preventing screen must be *behind* the tank, not against it, and preferably of white reflecting material on the face towards the sun. A sheet of glass painted white is usually excellent but may still admit too much light.

## LIGHT NEEDED BY PLANTS

The prime necessity is adequate light for the plants, as quite dull illumination is sufficient for most fishes. Plants, however, function and flourish only in good light, and many of them need bright light for much of the day to grow properly. Light of just sufficient intensity for comfortable reading is quite useless for them. The various species of *Cryptocoryne* and *Sagittaria* can take less illumination than the rest and should be used whenever there is doubt as to the brightness of the light in the tank. At the other extreme, plants like *Cabomba* and *Myriophyllum* grow stringy and drab and die off if not in bright light and become a menace instead of an ornament and a help in the tank. Only actively growing plants, and that means adequately lit plants, are an asset to the aquarium.

The light utilized by plants in photosynthesis is from the red end of the spectrum, and the growing habit of tinting the back and side glasses of tanks blue is to be avoided when oblique natural light of borderline intensity is employed. A significant amount of useful rays is removed in this manner, but the rays are not removed, of course, when the light comes from overhead and not through the glass.

When there is excess light, such as to cause a blanket of green algae over not only the glass but plants and rocks as well, it can always be cut down by shading. This shading is best applied to the windows admitting the light, as heat absorption which is likely to accompany the excessive light is avoided as explained above. If it must be applied to the tank, use white or light surfaces so as to reflect as much heat as possible and not to absorb it. Winter daylight in most parts of the world is not adequate for indoor tanks and should be supplemented with electric lighting.

## ARTIFICIAL LIGHT

Artificial light must be bright and close overhead. The light in an ordinary room is quite inadequate, even if the tank sits underneath the source of light, unless this is a veritable beacon. Either ordinary electric light bulbs or fluorescent lighting may be used. Fluorescent lights have the advantage already mentioned of causing little additional heat when this is not wanted. Whichever be the choice, it is usual to enclose the overhead tank lights in a reflector, which increases the light thrown into the tank and also prevents dazzle. Most reflectors are not of a very efficient design, and they also tend to decrease the life of incandescent bulbs, which get hotter when hooded over, so that aquarium toplights rather frequently need replacements, if not fluorescent.

The overhead lighting may be toward the front or back of the tank. Its appearance and the general direction of plant growth will differ in the two circumstances, and it all depends on which you like. The tank with front lighting tends to have a gloomy back and to give an impression of depth and spaciousness, but the plants at the back may not flourish too well after a period. The tank with back lighting has a fine background growth of plants and looks generally lighter and therefore rather less spacious and intriguing, and the fishes are transilluminated when they swim to the front. This gives an effect which depends on the fish; some look very pleasant and others lose effectiveness. On the whole, back lighting seems the less popular. A movable top light is the obvious solution.

## LIGHTING INTENSITY

With fluorescent lighting and a reflector of average efficiency, the following are the requirements of various tanks, assuming no help from even weak daylight:

| Tank Capacity liters | Usual depth, cm | Kilowatt-hours needed per day |
|---|---|---|
| 20 | 22 | 0.15 |
| 60 | 30 | 0.20 |
| 120 | 88 | 0.25 |
| 180 | 45 | 6.33 |
| 320 | 53 | 0.40 |
| 480 | 60 | 0.50 |

Translated into more useful terms, the figures in the last column multiplied by 100 give the wattage to employ, assuming ten hours per day of illumination. Thus, a 20-watt tube turned on for ten hours over a 60-liter tank is satisfactory, giving 0.2 kilowatt-hour per day.

Those familiar with the inverse square law may start to do a little figuring for themselves and wonder why a 180-liter tank, with twice the depth of a 20-liter tank, doesn't need four times the wattage instead of a mere two + times. There is a twofold reason. First, the difference in plant depth is not doubled because the tank depth is doubled. Plants right down on the gravel will be perhaps at about double the distance, but not the average plant leaf, which will often be able to reach just as near the bulb, whatever the tank depth. Second, the use of a reflector modifies the inverse square law and focuses the light into a beam or band, projecting it down into the tank and not allowing it to spread out as much as the light from a naked bulb. It also so happens that, even without an overhead reflector, the internal reflection from the inner faces of the glass prevents the escape of much of the light and aids the illumination of the deeper parts of the tank.

The figures recommended are thus a mixture of theory and experiment—mostly the latter. Although it would give about the same result to illuminate a 60-liter tank with 40 watts for five hours instead of with 20 watts for ten hours, it is best to use the weaker light and a longer period, since the fishes do better that way. If, on the other hand, it is desired to illuminate for a longer period, then 15 watts for 15 hours would be quite in order. There has been a lot of controversy about longer periods of illumination, extending even to *constant* illumination for 24 hours a day, and its effects on fishes, although there can seldom be any reason for wanting to illuminate adult fishes constantly, unless to supply oxygen via the plants in a very crowded tank. Adult fishes definitely rest in the dark, possibly because they can't see to do much else, but they probably do not sleep. There is no evidence known to the author that constant illumination harms them, apart from hearsay reports.

Fry, on the other hand, are sometimes given prolonged or constant lighting to keep them feeding and growing—which it certainly does, without obvious harm. In a fry-raising tank it would probably be a good idea to run at a higher total kilowatt-hours per day, as the fry are very actively consuming oxygen and producing waste, and the plants need to be in top form. A 30 to 50% increase seems in order.

# HEATING

As with lighting, electricity is so much more general and satisfactory for heating aquaria than any other method that oil and gas represent nothing more than auxiliary emergency measures. In fish rooms or houses, steam or hot water may, of course, be used. Electric heating has all the advantages—it may be left indefinitely without attention, it is clean, odorless, and comparatively cheap, and, most important, it does not have to be applied to the bottom of the tank and thus heat the roots of plants.

With electricity, a few simple definitions and formulas are helpful. With either alternating or direct current, the amount of electric energy used by a heater or any other apparatus is measured in watts. One watt is the amount of energy utilized when one ampere flows at a pressure of one volt. A thousand watts, one kilowatt, used for one hour gives the familiar unit of electricity, the kilowatt-hour. The heating capacity of a heater depends on its consumption of current; the higher the wattage, the more heat is produced. Typical heaters are rated at 12½, 25, 37½, 50, 75, 125, 150, 175, 200, and 250 watts, but other series are available at 10, 20, 30, 40, 50, 75, and 100 watts, so that it is possible to obtain a ready-made heater of almost any wattage required. This is important when different tanks are to be heated by separate heaters but all arc controlled by one thermostat.

The unit of resistance of a conductor is the ohm. It is related to watts, volts, and amperes so that:

$$\text{Current in amperes} = \frac{\text{volts}}{\text{ohms}}$$

$$\text{Watts} = \text{volts} \times \text{amperes}$$

$$\text{''} = \frac{(\text{volts})^2}{\text{ohms}}$$

The wattage of a heater of 500 ohms resistance when a 110-volt current is passed is therefore:

$$(110 \times 110)/500 = 24.2 \text{ watts}$$

Wire for use in heaters is always rated at a certain number of ohms per foot or per yard, so that the length required in a heater can be calculated if the current and the desired wattage are known.

$$\text{Ohms required} = \frac{(\text{volts})^2}{\text{watts}}$$

The heat loss from a heated tank depends mainly on the radiating, conducting, and evaporating surfaces of the tank, and on the difference between tank and air temperatures. Other things being equal, a small tank requires most heat per liter (more *watts* per liter) than a large tank because it loses heat more rapidly. In theory, we should expect the heat loss to be proportional to the surface area and, in similarly shaped tanks, to the square of any one dimension. Since the volume of such tanks is proportional to the cube of any one dimension, the number of watts per liter required for a given temperature to be maintained should be inversely proportional to the length or height of the tank. This is roughly borne out in practice and holds over a useful range of tank sizes. The rate of heat loss from similar tanks, other things being equal, is also approximately proportional to the square of the air-water temperature difference. Thus it takes about four times as much heating to keep a 10 °C difference as a 5 °C difference from the tank's surroundings. This is because the greater part of the heat loss does not occur by radiation or simple conduction, which follows a different law, but by convection and, in uncovered tanks, by evaporation. With low differences in temperature between tanks and their surroundings, the rate of heat loss follows much more nearly a square law than anything else, although this is *not* the relationship to be expected at greater temperature differences.

These observations may be translated to a few simple formulas, taking as standard a 60-liter covered tank kept at 10 °C above room temperature. This will usually be 60 cm long and it happens to require about 1 watt per liter, a total of 60 watts, to keep it at the stated temperature. In actual practice, a thermostat would be included to cut off the heat at a given point, say 24 °C, to allow for fluctuations in room temperature, and the room would have to fall below 14 °C for the tank temperature to start falling.

The watts per liter for tanks of the same general shape but of different sizes, all to be kept 10 °C above their surroundings, is given by:

$$\text{Watts per liter} = l_{60}/l_x$$

where $l_{60}$ = the length of the 60-liter tank (usually 60 cm), and $l_x$ = the length in cm of any other tank.

Thus, an 11-liter tank of 35 cm length requires not 1 watt per liter, but 1.7 watts (60/35 = 1.7 approx.), a total of 19 watts approx. The watts per gallon for the *same* tank, or others very similar to it, at different temperatures is given by:

$$\text{Watts per liter} = t^2/10^2 \text{ or } t^2/100$$

where $t$ is the temperature difference required.

Thus a 60-liter tank to be held at 15°C above its surroundings requires $15^2/100$ or 2.25 watts per liter, a total of 135 watts—more than double the requirement for a 10°C difference.

We can combine these formulas ao that the requirement of tanks of similar shape may be predicted. Almost no rectangular tanks likely to be used will differ enough to matter in actual fact:

$$\text{Watts per liter} = t^2 l_{60}/100 \; l_x$$

where the symbols have the meanings defined above.

From the above, we may deduce the wattage of heaters required under different conditions and the relative heater capacities required when one tank acts as a control for the others, some or all of which are of different liter capacities. The circuits which may be used in such linked tanks are discussed below.

The following table gives the information for a maximum rise of 10°C, i.e. the heaters would be adequate to raise the water in all tanks to 10°C above air temperature, but not more. The heating capacity needed for greater or lesser differences can be worked out as above. The tanks are assumed to be double cubes —i.e., a 60-liter measures 60x30x30cm, covered by a glass sheet. The last column of the table is of particular importance. Being calculated for a 10°C rise, it covers all normal requirements and is therefore a column of the heater wattages to be recommended for tanks of different sizes. These wattages give adequate heat but at the same time make it unlikely that the fishes will be cooked, even if the heater remains on when it should be switched off— either through a thermostatic fault or forgetfulness.

| Tank length, cm | Capacity, liters | Watts per liter | Approx. Total watts |
|---|---|---|---|
| 25 | 4 | 2.4 | 10 |
| 30 | 7 | 2.0 | 14 |
| 35 | 11 | 1.7 | 19 |
| 40 | 17 | 1.5 | 26 |
| 45 | 24 | 1.3 | 31 |
| 50 | 33 | 1.2 | 40 |
| 55 | 45 | 1.1 | 50 |
| 60 | 60 | 1.0 | 60 |
| 65 | 72 | 0.90 | 65 |
| 70 | 91 | 0.85 | 77 |
| 75 | 114 | 0.80 | 91 |
| 80 | 132 | 6.75 | 99 |
| 85 | 160 | 0.70 | 112 |
| 90 | 190 | 0.65 | 124 |
| 105 | 303 | 0.60 | 182 |
| 120 | 455 | 0.50 | 228 |

It should be noted that these figures are based on the assumption that the tanks are full of water. Planted tanks with sand and an air space will have less water in them, particularly small tanks, and, although the rocks and sand act in part as if they were water, the general effect is a reduction in equivalent water volume. For complete nicety of calculation, therefore, one might consider true water volumes, but this will rarely make as much as 1 °C difference to the result. In actuality the nearest available heater will have to be selected.

## TYPES OF HEATERS

Electric heaters are usually made of glass and they may be totally submersible or so constructed that their tops must not be placed under the water. Internally, the heater is essentially a heating coil wound on a ceramic or Pyrex glass form. This may be surrounded by a layer of fine sand or left bare inside the outer tube, which is sealed with a rubber bung or cap through which pass insulated flex wires. Submersible heaters are watertight; others are not, and so must stand vertically in the tanks with their tops out of water. The resistance wire, usually of thin nichrome or similar alloy, heats up as does an electric radiator element, and it is therefore necessary to make sure that the business part of the heater is covered by water or it will fuse. This wire is usually in the lower half of upright heaters, and tanks should never be allowed to fall below about two-thirds full for fear of heater trouble. For the same reason, care should be taken not to leave heaters on when emptying tanks, or to plug in a dry heater, or, worse still, to plunge it into water if it does get hot. Even Pyrex glass may not stand up to such treatment.

Glass heaters cannot be grounded as such, but the tank and the water in it can be grounded by placing an earth wire so that it contacts the metal frame if any *and* the water. Do not worry if a small bare copper wire touches the water, for the amount of metal is too small to produce ill effects in a freshwater tank, but not a marine one! However, most aquarists prefer to work in an earth-free situation, but should then avoid bare feet and wet floors!

Totally submersible heaters are popular, as they are not conspicuous and also because of the belief that they heat more efficiently. This is not correct; whether the heater stands upright or lies along the gravel, it causes a current of hot water to rise to the top of the tank and does not heat the water uniformly. The heater should never be buried in the gravel; if it is, it may fuse and it may also kill the neighboring plants.

As an alternative to the use of conventional heaters, rubber-covered or plastic-covered cable is available which may be laid along the base of the tank. It was originally designed for hothouse purposes but is quite suitable for the fish tank. There is no point in using electric heating below the base of tanks, as the great fault of other types of heating, the heating of the gravel, then occurs. When hot water or steam pipes are laid below, but not touching, tanks in a fish room, it is fortunate that much of the heating occurs as the hot air circulates up around the back and sides, so the actual floor heating effect is minimal and plant growth is usually satisfactory.

## THERMOSTATS

Although a low-wattage heater may in fact be used without any control on its output, it is usual and much safer to include a thermostat in the circuit. The almost universal type in aquaria is the bimetallic strip. This is a strip of two types of metal which expand at different rates with a rise in temperature, causing the strip to bend as the temperature rises. The strip carries the electric current, but at the critical temperature a terminal on the strip breaks contact with a terminal in the instrument and the current ceases to flow. As the tank cools again, contact is once again established. The "differential," as it is called, should not exceed 1 °C.

Various refinements make a good thermostat reliable and noiseless. It should have a magnetic "make," which means that the strip, once it gets near to completing the circuit, is snapped over into position by a small magnet, thus preventing sparking or arcing. The contacts should be of silver to prevent excessive wear, and there should be a condenser or capacitor to prevent radio interference. If it is not built into the instrument, it may be added afterwards quite easily; a suitable condenser is about 0.02 microfarad.

The thermostat is nearly always non-submersible if separate from the heater and is clipped onto the side of the tank. It has a glass body, with the works inside it, and a control which consists usually of a small adjustable screw with a non-conducting portion so that the operator can alter the setting of the bimetallic strip and hence the temperature of the tank. Often a pilot light is present which indicates when the thermostat is operating. There are more expensive models in which the thermostat proper is outside the tank feeling the temperature through the glass, or a temperature "feeler" is placed in the tank like a submersible heater. Combination models of thermostat-plus-heater are common and seem to be satisfactory. However, they can be used only in a single tank and hence each combination must be repeated for every additional tank.

The wattage of a thermostat is the number of watts it can safely control. A usual figure is 500 watts, but anything between 100 and 2,000 is available. A 500-watt thermostat may be used in conjunction with heaters totaling not more than 500 watts. It will often have a multiple plug, allowing several heaters to be plugged directly into it in parallel. Two 100-watt heaters in parallel will mean a current producing 200 watts through the thermostat, and so on, but it must be noted that two 100-watt heaters in series means only 50 watts through the thermostat, and an output of 25 watts per heater. This is important when using heaters in series.

160

## MULTIPLE CIRCUITS

The normal way of heating several tanks is to plug in suitable heaters to a thermostat placed in the smallest tank. This is because the smallest volume of water most rapidly loses and gains heat from its surroundings, and if a large tank housed the thermostat a small one might fluctuate too much. Conversely, this arrangement has the effect of controlling the temperature of the larger tanks (if there is a size difference) remarkably accurately. Although such an extremely even temperature is not really desirable, it is better than the alternative of widely varying small tanks. This is temperature control by heaters in parallel and is standard. The tanks that are all controlled by the same thermostat must be in reasonably similar situations if it is required that they shall be uniform in temperature. Otherwise, some will be hotter than others, although all may be within a reasonable range.

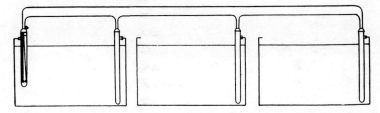

Heaters in series.

An alternative method is to use heaters in series. If a number of medium to large tanks are to be placed in such a circuit, the heaters may have to be made specially, since those available commercially will usually be of too high a resistance. A run of smallish tanks may be served by using high-wattage heaters in series. Thus, a single 200-watt heater running on 100 volts has a resistance of 60 ohms. If three such heaters are placed in series in three similar tanks, the total resistance is 180 ohms approximately, and the output is 66 watts or 22 watts per heater. This would be quite adequate for three 5-gallon tanks under normal conditions. However, the heaters will usually need to be rewound at least, or they may be made cheaply by anyone with adequate electrical knowledge. From the table the total required wattage is

161

determined (by interpolation if necessary), and the output from each heater will then be directly proportional to the resistance of its coils.

*Example:* Determine the resistance needed for heaters to serve six tanks of 20, 20, 40, 40, 60 and 100 liters capacity, all in series on 110 volts. (Interpolate in the table to determine the total watts needed for each tank).

The total wattage needed is:

| Tank Capacity | Watts Needed | No. of Tanks | Total watts |
|---------------|--------------|--------------|-------------|
| 20 | 28 | 2 | 56 |
| 40 | 44 | 2 | 88 |
| 60 | 60 | 1 | 60 |
| 100 | 86 | 1 | 86 |
| | | | Total 290 |

Ohms required (total) = (volts)$^2$/watts = 12,100/290 = 41.7 ohms.

This total of 41.7 ohms must be proportioned as is the wattage required from each heater, so for ease of calculation we divide it once more by 290 to get the number of ohms per watt of output; this is 41.7/290, or 0.144 ohms per watt.

The required number of ohms for each of the six heaters is therefore: 4.0, 4.0, 6.3, 6.3, 8.6 and 12.3 (= 41.4 ohms - near enough!).

There are several advantages in having heaters in series. First, the voltage drop across any one heater is small, and the danger of a short is correspondingly low. Second, the element may be made of stout, relatively low-resistance wire, since a low total resistance is usually needed, and so the danger of fusing is almost nil. Third (and this is rather a subtle one), when specially made heaters are used, there is not only little chance of chilling the fishes but no chance of cooking them, owing to the heater in the control tank fusing, for if *any* heater fuses all of them are out of action. With heaters in parallel, the failure of the heater in the same tank as the thermostat results in the thermostat's remaining permanently closed and thus overheating all other tanks on the same circuit. Unless heaters of minimum necessary capacity are being used, this may kill all the remaining fishes.

## CONTROLLED DIFFERENCES IN TANK TEMPERATURE

Running a series of tanks from the same thermostat does not preclude having differences in temperature purposely arranged, as long as the external temperature does not rise above that of the control tank for some appreciable time. It will be obvious that some tanks can be made purposely hotter than others by giving them more powerful heaters, but further thought will show that the difference will increase, the lower the external temperature. Suppose that we have two similar 60-liter tanks and give one of them a 60-watt heater and the other a 90-watt heater. At one extreme, when tank one, with 60 watts, is 10 °C above the room temperature, tank two will be about 13 °C above. At the other, when the room temperature has risen to, say, 24 °C and tank one is at the same temperature and so the thermostat opens permanently, tank two is no longer heated either and so falls gradually to 24 °C as well. On the whole, however, tank two will be above tank one to a useful degree for, say, spawning purposes.

With uniform heaters, or with heaters designed to give uniform temperatures in different-size tanks, much can be done by adjusting water levels and by tight covering. Covering a tank tightly raises its temperature by about 2 °C above that of a similar tank left uncovered, under average conditions, when a fair amount of heat is being applied. This is mainly because most of the heat loss by evaporation is prevented. Lowering the water by a safe margin—say not more than to two-thirds—can do as much or even more, so that these two methods together can give fair flexibility. By using screen covers, glass covers, partial covers, and different water levels, a range of temperatures of from about 22° to 27 °C is possible, and this is about all that is usually required. Another factor that may be introduced is aeration, as the aerated tank is not only more uniform in temperature throughout because of the water movement but it also loses heat more rapidly. An uncovered, briskly aerated tank in a cool room can be 5 °C lower than another which is tightly covered, has a lower water level, and has the same number of watts supplied to it. This applies to the temperature taken about half-way up the tank in both cases, and the surface of the covered tank will be even hotter.

Aeration stones are manufactured in different shapes and sizes. Keep a few spare airstones for immediate replacement of clogged or damaged ones.

**Left:** The vibrator pump is inexpensive, efficient, powerful and requires very little electricity to run. Because of its simple construction, breakdowns are easy to repair. **Right:** Understandably, large freshwater tanks and almost all marine tanks can benefit from a power filter.

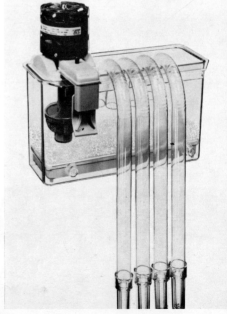

# CHAPTER SEVEN
## Aeration, Filtration, and Circulation of the Water

There are probably more misconceptions about aeration than about any other section of aquarium lore; indeed, as we do not fully understand the effects of aeration in relation to the action of plants, etc., this is not surprising. We do know, however, that aeration does *not* force air (or oxygen) into solution in the water, which is the most popular misconception. Nor, under usual conditions, is much oxygen absorbed from the bubbles themselves; they merely serve to stir the water, and a small propeller would perform the same function. Oddly enough, this method never seems to be employed. It would therefore be superfluous to use oxygen rather than air, and certainly much more expensive, unless such a fine jet at powerful pressure were used that the tank looked like a soda fountain in action.

The accounts in the literature of the rate at which aeration of different types brings about the solution of oxygen from the air in water that is deficient in oxygen are conflicting. The general conclusion seems to be that it is not as efficient as we have tended to think, some investigators finding that only very brisk bubbling from several aerating stones at once will bring a tank up to 75% saturation within 30 minutes. The normal rate of aeration—a mild trickle from one stone—was found to be ineffective even within several hours. This need not alarm us unduly, because the rate at which carbon dioxide needs to be "blown off" is quite low, and this is probably the most important factor. The fact remains that quite mild aeration about doubles the fish capacity of a tank, and although brisk, boiling aeration might quadruple it or even much more as far as air content is concerned, other factors would prevent us from trying to crowd our tanks so much. Chief among these would be pollution from excessive fecal and other matter.

### AERATION STONES

The usual method of aeration is to force air through a porous "stone" at the bottom of the tank. Such a stone may be made of various substances, from fused glass or natural minerals to leather, wooden or felt barriers on a metal head. Carborundum stones give about the finest bubbles but also need the most powerful air pressure, so that only the larger sized pumps are satisfactory for their use. All stones tend to clog, especially when not used at much pressure, and they should occasionally be removed, thoroughly dried (even baked), and reset. When they are first used or re-used, it is advisable to send a brisk jet of air through them for a few hours, and when this is turned down a fine spray of bubbles is usually the result.

Fine plastic tubing is used to lead air from the pump to the stone or stones, and various connecting pieces, valves, and clips to control the rate of air flow are on the market. Even dust filters for inserting into the air line are available, also pressure gauges, but the average aquarist will not find them of much help.

## FACTORS AFFECTING EFFICIENCY

Experience shows that with reasonably small bubbles, of an average diameter of about 1 mm or less, an aerating stone delivering 30 ml of air per minute is adequate in a 60-liter tank. This observation is really of great interest, for it demonstrates the fact that adequate aeration does not work by simple bubble-water interchange, as the surface of the bubbles exposed to the water at any one moment is only about 80 cm², assuming a bubble diameter of 1 mm and a period of four seconds for a bubble to travel from bottom to top of the tank. As the bubble size decreases (a really first-class stone can give bubbles of less than 0.25 mm in diameter), the surface exposed by the bubbles rapidly increases, for not only is it greater per ml of air, but also the bubbles take longer to reach the surface. With 0.25 mm bubbles, which take some 10 to 15 seconds to travel up through the water, the area exposed is 800 to 1200 cm², but even then it is less than the normal surface area of the tank (1800 cm²). With such fine bubbles, the water looks quite cloudy over the stone, for at any one moment as many as 1 million are suspended in the water. When the bubble diameter is 1 mm, a mere 2,000 odd are seen at once. Furthermore, such very fine bubbles do not move water so much and do not disturb the surface of the water, and thus the surface interchange is little affected; therefore the effects of very fine subdivision of the same volume of air may not be as good as rather coarser subdivision. It is the opinion of some experts that a bubble diameter of about 0.8 mm is the best.

Deep tanks gain relatively more from aeration than do shallower tanks, for not only are they in more need of it but, since the bubbles take longer to rise to the surface, they cause more effective stirring of the water and a brisker surface interchange.

## TYPES OF AIR PUMPS

The commonest aerator is a pump, operated electrically. Pumps are designed to deliver anything from 200 to 4,000 ml of air per minute and thus operate from a few to a hundred stones. The electrical consumption of the most powerful is quite small, no more than 30 or 40 watts; the smaller pumps take as little as 3 watts and thus cost next to nothing to run. In fact, if an electric meter is not in first-class order, a 3-watt pump working alone does not move it.

Pumps may be of single or multicylinder type, or without cylinders at all, operated by a vibrating diaphragm. Those without cylinders are the cheapest to run and have been perfected by a number of manufacturers to such a stage that they are often preferred to the older cylinder pumps. They do not require oiling and are more silent, or should be, but they are less durable and must be placed above the level of water in any tank they supply or water may run back into the pump. On the other hand, they do not reverse, as do some pumps of conventional design, and so cannot actively suck the water into themselves.

Air may be compressed into drums, and this can last for quite a time. Even a 20-liter drum pumped up to a pressure of one atmosphere (1 kg per cm²), half the pressure in a car tire, will deliver a total of about 18,000 ml of air. This is enough to operate an aeration stone for about ten hours, but the air would not flow at a uniform rate throughout this period. A better arrangement is to have water flowing from one reservoir to another, displacing air at a more uniform pressure throughout the period covered. A more efficient, small electric pump is a much easier solution and doesn't cost very much.

## OTHER AERATION METHODS

Various forms of spray or drip have often been used for aerating tank water. A steady drip, which causes small quivering waves to run over the surface of the water, is quite an efficient means of aeration when run at the rate of about one drop per second. This will use up about 4 liters per day, so that in the average aquarium there need be no provision for overflow, but if this is desired or if a faster drip is used, it is easy to provide.

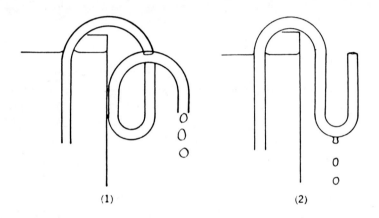

(1)                    (2)

Constant level siphons.

The best device is the constant level siphon, which operates only when the water rises above a pre-arranged level, yet does not empty itself and becomes functionless when the flow ceases. There are two types, both with essentially the same design. When the water level in the tank drops to that of the right-hand arm of the siphon, or of the hole in the top bend of the alternative design, the flow ceases, but it starts again when the level goes higher. The siphon may have a plug of filter wool or other device fitted so that small fishes do not escape, but in actual fact they rarely do so, even when the tube is left open.

Instead of a drip, a fountain may be used, but this requires a lot of water. Nothing less than a flow of 160 to 200-liters a day will be any good, so that a return pump is necessary to provide the fountainhead. Therefore the pump may as well be used in the first place as the primary source of aeration. However, in suitable surroundings a fountain looks very attractive. The tank must be large and the nozzle bore very small, so that a very fine jet is sent at least a few centimeters into the air, to fall back onto the water surface in small drops. The aerating effect is excellent, and the rate of flow of water is usually such that it all circulates within a few hours and comes into contact with the air in droplet form.

An electric fan playing on the surface of the water is also an excellent aerator, causing the water to circulate quite briskly across the top of the tank and then down away from the air current.

## PUMPING WATER

If large volumes of water are to be moved, particularly from one level to another which is several feet higher, a water pump as such is necessary. For smaller jobs, involving a water lift of not more than a few cm and a volume of not more than about 400 liters a day (which is really quite a lot), an air pump may be used.

A stream of air is injected from a small-bore air line into a vertical water line of rather larger bore. This breaks the water and air up into bubbles, and they are carried upwards together. The air can lift the water some 10 to 12 cm above tank level, but efficient working requires a small rise only, unless a rather complicated arrangement of tubing is erected beside the tank. Older water lifts used the air to push the water over from one container to another —usually from a tank to a filter carton or vice versa.

A useful size for the air tube in such instruments is 3 mm, and for the water line 5 mm, both internal diameter. Both are commonly made of glass or plastic, but any other convenient substance may be used, as long as there is no danger of water poisoning. In ordinary use, such an air lift uses five to ten times the air that is needed by an aeration stone.

It will be apparent that in any system of connected vessels it is necessary to install only one water lift operated as above, since siphon tubes may be used for all other connections. These tubes will ensure a flow of water such that all levels tend to be equal and will rapidly become equal once the pump is stopped. To ensure that a siphon does not cease to function, both arms must dip below the water surface, and in any setup where the blocking of a siphon tube could be disastrous two should be installed in parallel. It is a much wiser precaution to arrange all systems so that such a blockage does not do any damage. Thus, a water lift from one tank to another should never draw water from far below the surface, so that should a return siphon become blocked, water in the tank from which it is being actively pumped will not be sucked dangerously low.

Water pumps are available commercially of almost any capacity required, and are used in all kinds of power filtration, particularly in marine aquaria, where brisk water movement and aeration are desired. They may pump water into filters of various types or may be used to pump water from a filter back into the tank, setting up a stream of purified and/or aerated water. Some are submersible, others must sit over or below the tank, according to whether or not they are self-priming. The best types (not necessarily the most expensive) avoid contact of anything but plastic or glass with the water—particularly necessary with salt water.

In an aquarium of around 100-liter capacity, a water pump capable of pumping 300 to 400 liters an hour will turn the water over several times an hour through a filter of one kind or another and create a small and useful current in the tank. Attached to an undergravel filter, it will pull about the right amount of water through it per hour to achieve optimal biological filtration. Other tanks should be serviced proportionately.

## FILTERS

Filters use an air or water pump to shift water from the tank into a smaller container or from the container back into the tank, the other part of the water lift being by siphon. Power filters force water through a filter bed or capsule and back into the tank all in one action. They employ a closed water-tight system to do this. A simple filter may be constructed from a glass or other container (plastic is easiest to work) by boring a set of small holes in the base and clipping it onto the inside of the tank. Water is then pumped into the container, passes through a bed of filter wool or other material, and out again into the tank. When water is pumped from the filter back to the tank, the same design can be used; the water will pass up through the holes in the bottom and through the filter. This, however, tends to raise the filtering medium, and the water passes beside it more than through it, and so the direction of flow is reversed by sucking water from the bottom of the filter, dispensing with a pierced base, and siphoning water from the tank into the top of the filter. A very efficient type of filter, which also aerates effectively, sits on the bottom and sends a current of air and water up through a central tube by means of an air stone at the base. Water enters at the gridded top of the filter and passes through a bed of filter material before reaching the base of the filter.

Another type, which is much more usual, may be placed outside the tank, clipped onto the side or even on a separate stand. The siphon which carries aquarium water into the filter is provided with a "starter" consisting of a small rubber ball which, when compressed, starts the filter without the operator having to suck at the tube or remove it and fill it with water. The principle is quite simple. There is a short tube from the ball which runs with the short arm of the siphon almost to the end. The ball is squeezed and held while the first finger of the other hand is placed over the two tubes at the same time. When this finger is released the ball springs back to its normal shape and sucks water over momentarily, sufficient to start the siphon as long as there is only a short lift to be overcome, not more than 1 to 2 cm usually.

It is common practice to place granular activated charcoal at the base of the filter, then a layer of wool, through which the water first passes. The wool removes any grosser debris or particles, and the activated charcoal absorbs small impurities and also actively soaks up some dissolved material as well as actual suspended matter. Both should be replaced frequently enough to prevent exhaustion or blockage, and if this is done the filter rarely gives trouble. The water intake may be placed at a distance from the filter—perhaps in a front corner with the gravel so sloped that waste matter tends to collect there and be transported to the filter. Many filters have adjustable intake siphons to cope with differing aquarium depths and other dimensions. Others have more than one chamber, so that the water first passes through a wool bed and then separately through a charcoal bed, and perhaps through a bed of crystals designed to adjust the pH.

Power filters are expensive and are often used intermittently on any one tank to clear it up rapidly and then moved on to another tank. They may be equipped with removable capsules which clean up the water very efficiently but must be frequently changed, or they may force the water through very fine sand or diatomaceous earth, which collects anything down to bacteria and so helps to combat disease. Such filters usually employ conventional water pumps, but less forceful versions are available with magnetic drives, so that nothing but a magnetically driven disc enclosed in plastic touches the water. This type of impellor is not powerful enough for capsules or diatomaceous earth.

## UNDERGRAVEL FILTERS

Undergravel filters of various types have become very popular, in particular for marine aquaria. Such a filter consists of a perforated plate, usually of plastic, or a series of perforated tubes

Undergravel filters are useful in both freshwater and marine tanks. Separate units permit placement of the plates either close together as shown or apart with a space between them.

Activated granular charcoal is marketed not only in loose form, but also as inserts or cartridges that can be replaced conveniently at regular intervals.

A diatom filter is very effective in clearing clouded water and removing parasites and bacteria from infected water.

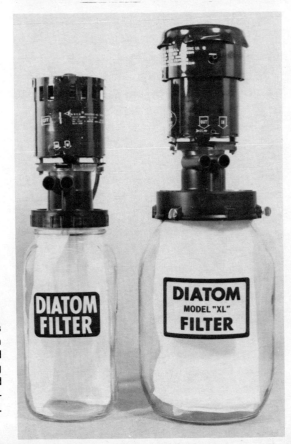

placed beneath the layer of gravel at the bottom of the tank. The plate is raised up about 1 cm from the tank base and connected to one or more uplift tubes which pump the water back towards the surface of the tank or into another filter if desired. The uplift tubes may be powered by airlifts (most usual) or by a water pump. A large tank may have several such plates, which in a freshwater tank need not cover the entire base, but which should do so in a marine tank.

With an undergravel filter, all of the water in the aquarium passes down through the gravel, which should be of the usual 5-7.5 cm depth, and is filtered relatively slowly (because of the large area of gravel) but efficiently before being returned to the tank. A good design turns the water over minimally about twice the total volume per hour. Some designs use a reverse flow system, pumping the water *upwards* through the gravel, but it is not clear how advantageous this may be.

The great advantage of undergravel filtration is the provision of a large filter bed in which bacteria grow to establish the biological cycle, particularly the nitrogen cycles, referred to above. In an ordinary filter, if the materials are not changed too often—as they may have to be because of clogging—a similar colony of bacteria may start up, but it will not have the massive substrate or time to become properly established, so that the extent to which a filter becomes biologically active may be very limited. Also, activated charcoal or even resins, when coated with bacteria, lose their original function and are likely to be replaced. So, in tanks without a subgravel filter, the nitrogen cycle depends on bacteria coating surfaces, including surface gravel only, and may be poorly established. This is more important in marine tanks than in freshwater tanks, where the action of plants is usually helping out.

Clearly, the efficiency of an undergravel filter depends on gravel size and depth and rate of flow. Very fine gravel—sand— is likely to clog rapidly, and very coarse gravel is too inefficient. To hold plants and to give an optimum life with at most occasional partial replacement, a gravel size of 2 to 5 mm, best as a mixture of sizes, is about the optimum. This is true of marine tanks as well. It is best never to replace all of the gravel, just siphon off any clogged areas or even just stir it up to get better filtration if there are signs of clogging (air uplifts "gurgling" or water pumps sucking dry).

Not all plants approve of undergravel filtration as it aerates their roots too much. There are two solutions in the freshwater aquarium. Either cover only part of the base with the filter, usually only the front or center front, or turn the filter off for part of the time. The first suggestion is best, as filtration continues without interruption and forgetting to turn it on and off is not at risk. Also, it does harm to the bacteria to leave them unsupplied with fresh water for any length of time—some say even as short as two hours. The center front of a tank is usually unplanted anyway. In a marine tank the problem does not arise.

## CIRCULATION SYSTEMS

The various devices so far described in this chapter may be used for circulating the water through a series of tanks, with or without the inclusion of a filter. It is unusual to circulate fresh water, but quite the reverse is true with salt water. The single saltwater tank is usually filtered and aerated by stones in addition, but when a number of tanks are run it is usual to circulate the sea water through these, through a separate large filter, then often into a reservoir, which may be much larger than any of the tanks, and then back to the tanks. The water is best filtered before it joins the reservoir, and best circulated to the tanks separately, so that they are in parallel and not in series. In that way an individual tank does not donate its water, possibly infected, to another tank before filtration. The same principle may naturally be used with a single tank if it is felt necessary.

The danger of circulation is the spread of infection. The filter may not trap germs efficiently, and any infection may rapidly spread from the tank of origin to all the others. Yet, in marine tanks the benefit of circulation is so great that it is worth the risk, for the fishes may be in such better health that their resistance to disease more than makes up for this greater chance of their being exposed to it. It is always used in public aquaria.

In freshwater tanks, circulation has been used, on a kind of sewage farm principle, to demonstrate the biology of the aquarium, and the system has been adapted for fishroom use by a few enthusiasts. It is a complex arrangement, requiring batteries of tanks devoted to the disposal of waste by microorganisms and invertebrates, and aeration, filtration, and final recirculation of the water through the fish tanks. For class work in biology, nothing could give a better demonstration of the natural processes which occur in the pond or the healthy tank, but as a method for the routine purification of water it is a little too much, in the author's opinion, and also too likely to go wrong unless in expert hands. The undergravel filter is of course an example in miniature of the same principles.

## OTHER EQUIPMENT

There is a great variety of equipment available, much of it designed for marine aquaria and therefore not described here. For example, ultraviolet sterilizers, protein skimmers and the like are rarely used in fresh-water tanks.

# CHAPTER EIGHT

## Aquarium Rooms and Breeding Batteries

Sooner or later the keen aquarist decides that he must have a room or separate house set apart for his fishes. By this time he will usually have a dozen tanks or more in odd corners all over the house or perhaps concentrated in one section where they tend to spread out in an alarming manner. He will be getting tired of makeshift arrangements, water on the carpets, and perhaps a mounting electricity bill which could be much reduced by heating and lighting all the tanks in a confined space by a really efficient system.

When this stage is reached it is best to find or provide the space to be devoted to fishes, and then to plan very carefully how to utilize it to best advantage. It is best not to decide that the room shall house, say, 40 tanks and then go out and place an order for the lot, plus shelving or stands and all the rest of the paraphernalia. It may be very depressing when it arrives, and so will be the bill. It is much better, instead, to build the room up slowly, although with a set plan (which may well undergo many improvements as experience is gained). By this method, the tanks, the plants, and the fishes keep pace, so that as new types are acquired and bred, they can be accommodated and shown to good advantage. Plants can be taken from existing tanks and set into the new ones, and in the course of perhaps a year the room will be a fully going concern.

### HEATING AND HEAT CONSERVATION

The tropical aquarium room is usually heated as a unit, by hot pipes or electricity. This has the advantage that thermostating of the whole room is simpler, and electric heating may be by tubular attachments, radiators, radiation panels, or by the new methods of cable heating.

If electricity is used for heating the fish room, it is, however, the author's opinion that the most sensible place to put it is into the tanks, by immersion heaters. Less current is thereby wasted heating the air of the room, and greater comfort is achieved for the operator, who does not have to work in the hothouse atmosphere that develops when the room heats the tanks, instead of the tanks heating the room. With such an arrangement and with 30 or 40 fair-sized tanks receiving a total of perhaps 2 or 3 kilowatts much of the time, the room is pleasantly heated and additional tanks for all but the tenderest species can be used without separate heating elements. A room in the author's home measuring 3.6x4.3 m approximately in floor area and containing some 1500 liters of water heated to about 24 °C was rarely below 18 °C, even when the outside temperature was 7 °C.

In temperate regions, where the temperature is likely to be freezing outside or even to drop much more severely, it is almost essential to insulate the tropical fish room by any of the common methods used for home insulation. Much heat is lost from the top of such rooms, and it will pay to give particular attention to this factor, double-glassing skylights, for instance, even if lower windows are left single. As we saw when discussing heat loss from a single aquarium, the rate at which heat is lost mounts as the difference between inside and outside temperature increases, more rapidly than the difference itself, so that rooms with a very large drop from inside to outside must be insulated as efficiently as possible. This is just as important when the source of heat is fed into the aquaria, for the ultimate loss is to the exterior of the tank room.

It is common practice to make floor pools, and even some tanks, from concrete or bricks covered by cement. These can be more efficiently made from aerated concrete, which can be bought in blocks and is a very efficient insulator. Covering such pools or large tanks, particularly at night, is also important. Removable night covers may be of wood or wood substitute, but any permanent covers must admit light. Floor tanks or pools present peculiar difficulties, as they do not receive so much heat from the surroundings in a thermostated or circulator-heated room and are not often heated by immersion elements. They have therefore a particular tendency to become or even to remain too cool and should be carefully watched as they may be a source of outbreaks of disease in tropicals.

## LIGHTING ARRANGEMENTS

If possible, overhead light should be admitted in excess of side light and may even be the only source of light. In temperate regions, half to all of the roof of a fish room should be of glass, which can be suitably shaded when necessary in summer, preferably by adjustable louver-type shades. In winter, all the light available will be welcome. In warmer climates, a surprisingly small amount of light needs to be admitted, and if top light alone is to be used it will be sufficient in latitudes of 25 to 40 degrees to have about one-fifth to one-fourth glass and three-fourths to four-fifths solid roof; in the tropics even less glass is sufficient.

An excess of light is not particularly harmful as such, but it is a nuisance if it causes overgrowth of algae, green water, and excessive plant growth in general. The biggest trouble, however, is the overheating which occurs in warmer climates when too much glass is used. Glass has the valuable property, when used in moderation, of admitting the heat rays of the sun but retaining the lower-temperature radiation from warm objects inside the room. It therefore acts as a heat trap, well-known to gardeners, and can cook fish in a greenhouse with great efficiency. Otherwise, glass is not a very good insulator and *conducts* heat fairly well, although it does not readily transmit the longer heat waves, to which it is opaque. Quite thick glass—2.5 cm or so—is needed for good insulation, or much cheaper double glass with an insulating air space of 2.5 cm or even less.

If the room has no separate roof, best use must be made of the windows. It will be found that the tanks nearest the windows get too much light, whereas those farthest off probably get too little and also get it too obliquely. Much can be done by shading those tanks which need it and by painting and keeping the upper part of the room white. Next best to overhead light is diffuse light, which doesn't come from any particular direction; this is attained by adequate ceiling and upper-wall reflection.

So far, we have considered the use of daylight. This may need to be supplemented with artificial light in the darker parts of a room which does not have skylights, or, if cost is no object, electric light may be used almost exclusively. If it is, there is much to be said in favor of fluorescent lighting, for there will need to be plenty of light. It will probably not be desirable to illuminate each tank separately, if only because of the cost and awkwardness when tanks are in tiers or banks. Instead, really powerful overhead lighting is needed, and in order not to be a source of unwanted heat in already hot weather, fluorescent tubes are almost mandatory. Fitted with good reflectors and placed above the tanks at a distance of 30 to 90 cm from the tank surface, something in the neighborhood of 60 watts of warm white fluorescent lighting is needed per meter run of tanks, to be used ten hours a day. The lower tanks in a fish room will be a bit bleak and may need supplementary light unless there is plenty of cross-illumination from several lights in different parts of the room.

In addition to the general overhead lighting it will be necessary to provide for one or two additional movable lamps which can be placed over or behind tanks for special observation or for the encouragement of plants or for spawning the fishes. A generous allowance of electric outlets should therefore be planned.

## THE TANKS

Tanks may be arranged in strictly vertical tiers, or they may be staggered in such fashion that they receive adequate top light and may easily be serviced. The only reason for a vertical arrangement with each row directly above the one below it would seem to be the conservation of space, as there is otherwise little in its favor. Not only do the tanks receive less natural light, and that in part from the wrong angle, but also the rows must be spaced fairly wide apart, so that there is room above each tank to get at it, to insert a light or a net and the arm when needed. This means at least 15 and preferably 20 cm between the top of one tank and the bottom of the next.

With a staggered arrangement, there need be little space between successive rows, or even none at all if the base of one tank clears or nearly clears the top of the tank below. When there is complete clearance, it looks very neat to overlap the tanks slightly so that the top of one hides the lower edge of the next above it. If the tanks are large, or rather wide from back to front, this arrangement makes the topmost tank difficult to service, and the best general arrangement is a moderate horizontal overlap which leaves at least two-thirds of each tank top exposed. Such a plan allows four rows of small to average-sized tanks, with the lowest 60 cm clear of the floor and the top of the highest still within arm's reach. If the stands or shelves holding the tanks are against the wall, there is room to squeeze behind and attend to any trouble; if they are in the center of the room, there is ample room to get below the double set of tiers that will normally be set up.

It is best to leave spaces between tanks on the same shelf; 10 cm is enough. They may then be transilluminated easily for spotting fry, and the arm can be inserted between them when fixing the various auxiliary gadgets with which one is always experimenting. The most satisfactory type of shelving, which can be rapidly erected and dismantled for storage, is one of the heavy-duty angle-iron utility shelvings. These are supplied in various lengths with supplies of nuts and bolts, and they are readily cut with a hacksaw to any desired length. Their strength is usually sufficient to support up to 45 cm of water per shelf, with supports at 120 cm intervals; more water can be supported if there are more upright members.

If a room inside the house is adapted as a fish room, do not neglect to obtain advice on the load-bearing capacity of the floor. Water is extremely weighty in the masses likely to be housed in a fair-sized room, which may not be designed to support a constant dead weight of perhaps 3 to 4 tons. An outside or ground-level room with concrete floor pools may carry up to 10 to 12 tons of water, but this is easily taken care of when laying the floor in the first place.

## AERATION

A fish room is best fitted with a central aeration system, with a reliable pump of adequate capacity for all needs—which does not necessarily mean aeration to all tanks. If the room is purely for exhibition purposes and not for breeding or other more experimental work, the aeration lines may be cunningly concealed

181

behind stands and run under the gravel of the tanks to stones. If, as is more often the case, the purpose of the room is more mutable, with aeration needed now here and now there and with some tanks likely to be emptied and shifted at frequent intervals, then a more workmanlike arrangement is best, with loose aeration lines which can be placed elsewhere in a few minutes.

A good plan is to run as many of the electricity and air lines as possible above the tanks, on the ceiling or high up on the walls. This keeps them out of the way, easy to get at, and safer than they otherwise would be.

## WATER AND DRAINAGE

It pays in trouble saved to lay water from the mains to the fish room and to put in drainage. Some even prefer to have a waste pipe running below each rack of tanks with small holes so that a siphon tube can be inserted at any point and water run off to the outside or into a receptacle for storage. It is quite satisfactory, however, to have a tap over a waste line in a corner of the room and a hose running to any part of the room with a corresponding siphon hose which is run into the drain. As an alternative, incoming water may run into a cistern placed high on the wall, so that a head of water exists to any tank. If the cistern is of good size, say 100 liters at least, it will contain sufficient conditioned water at the right temperature to meet any normal requirement and will automatically top up as water is drawn off. If this plan is not used, and if the local water supply is dangerous without maturation, then a storage tank of some kind, perhaps one of the aquaria themselves, must be pressed into service. Up to 10% of winter or 25% of summer tap water is safe without any maturation, even in the most highly chlorinated localities.

## QUARANTINE TANKS

The wise aquarist will maintain strict quarantine rules in his fish room. The quarantine tanks need not always be the same tanks, though it is perhaps best if they are, so that you don't forget which tank is in quarantine. If different tanks are used at different times it is a good plan to stick a readily noticed label on the glass or even to color the water with a little methylene blue or brilliant green, which will do no harm and may do good.

A quarantine tank must be tightly covered, and it should be separately serviced from the rest. No nets or instruments of any kind—including fingers, thermometers, and siphons—may be used in the tank without immediate and thorough washing, or, better still, sterilization in the case of instruments and nets. The best medium for sterilization is boiling water for half a minute or hot water (70 °C) for five to ten minutes, which will kill most things that are undesirable.

Fishes newly received should remain in quarantine for at least two weeks, preferably three weeks if the temperature is not above 20 °C. They should be carefully watched and any signs of disease treated immediately. Do not, on the other hand, treat without cause, as many treatments weaken the fishes and are harmful, although necessary for disease eradication. At the end of the quarantine period it is not advisable to put the new fishes into a community of others even then, for they are still likely to be carrying diseases which they do not show but which others will contract. The best way to test for this is to place a spare fish in with them—this can be done straight away while they are in quarantine—and see if it also remains healthy. This extra measure of precaution has saved the author from probable disaster several times. The common guppy is not a good subject, as it is tough and resistant to some ills and does not show white spot very noticeably, even though it is very susceptible and often dies of it. A spare platy or characin is much better, and since white spot and velvet are the diseases most to be guarded against it pays to recall that *Hemigrammus ocellifer* and *Hyphessobrycon flammeus* seem particularly susceptible to white spot and are therefore excellent test subjects. Another good test fish is *Puntius nigrofasciatus*, while *Brachydanio rerio* is very susceptible to velvet.

Isolation tanks for fishes removed from communities because of disease or injury should be similarly run, with the exception that the inmates will usually be receiving treatment. Both quarantine and isolation tanks are best left unplanted and bare, save for a handful of loose plants—any will do, but those naturally without roots such as *Ceratophyllum* or *Nitella* look best. Then, if treatment is needed, there will be less chance of the drugs being destroyed by mulm or other tank contents, and the job of cleaning and sterilizing afterwards will be much easier. These tanks should also be small ones, which have thinner glass and so can be sterilized with hot water, which take a small water volume so that the amount of drug needed is less, and which can more readily be shifted and filled and emptied without much danger of developing a leak. Tanks of 10 to 20 liters capacity are about right; even smaller tanks may be used for individuals or pairs receiving treatment.

## BREEDING BATTERIES

A battery of smallish unplanted tanks is also best for breeding most species. These tanks can also be sterilized easily and moved about, and if they are kept in a battery under a common thermostat the rather higher temperature appropriate to breeding in most tropicals and for raising fry is provided to all tanks. The various methods for preparing and using these tanks are described in the chapters concerned with breeding. To some, the sterilized, almost bare and ugly-looking breeding tank advocated here may seem rather a shame, and it also may be something of a surprise to those who have been used to providing the first food by means of natural infusorial growth in the breeding tank itself. However, the results achieved by more rigorous and scientific methods are also a surprise to the older school of breeders, many of whom were content with growing perhaps 20 or 30 young anabantids from a spawning instead of several hundred to a thousand or so. Such results should be fairly regularly achieved when desired and with fully adult fishes as parents.

# CHAPTER NINE

## Breeding Live-bearers

The live-bearing fishes (Poeciliidae) are the easiest of all aquarium fishes to breed; indeed, the only problem usually encountered is that of saving the young from the cannibalism of their parents. They breed all the year 'round if kept warm and well lighted, but a deficiency of either light or warmth can arrest reproduction completely, as also can highly acid water. Within the temperature range 20° to 27°C, the only influence of heat is to shorten the period of gestation.

Different live-bearer species require different water conditions, but in general alkaline water is preferable, with quite high salinity (not necessarily hardness) for some species. It is best to consult specialized books if you want to succeed with a particular unusual species, although guppies, platies, swordtails and mollies almost have to be *stopped* from breeding unless in very unsuitable conditions. Some guppy breeders prefer slightly acid water, but it isn't essential, whereas mollies are very unhappy unless in alkaline conditions, and both they and guppies can breed in full-strength sea water. This is not true of swords, platies, or of most other live-bearers.

Despite the excellence of many prepared foods, rather surprising reports have been published showing that adult guppies should be fed live or recently living foods for highest fertility. Fry numbers in the order of 100-200 were achieved in one experiment with fresh or frozen chopped earthworms, beef heart or tubifex, whereas flakes or granular foods and even freeze-dried brine shrimp or tubifex gave only 40 or 50 young per litter. White worms, despite being a popular live food, when fed exclusively resulted in litters averaging only 16 young! Clearly a mixed diet with plenty of "meaty" content and live foods is to be recommended in our present state of knowledge.

### SEX IN LIVE-BEARERS

Fortunately, the differentiation of sexes is easy in mature fishes of this family. The males characteristically possess a gonopodium, an organ of copulation which is formed from the modified anal fin. There is often a large difference in the size of the sexes, males being smaller. This is particularly obvious in the guppy, in which the male is also highly colored and may have long and variously shaped decorative fins, whereas the female is normally drab. Markedly smaller males also occur in *Poecilia vivipara, Quintana atrizona, Phallichthys amates, Heterandria bimaculata, Heterandria formosa* and *Gambusia affinis.* In most other aquarium live-bearer species the male is usually the smaller fish. In the important swordtails, platies, and mollies, the difference in sex size disappears, and both sexes show a variety of colors, except in *Xiphophorus variatus,* which has rather drab females.

Much more is known about the inheritance of color and color variations in the platies, swordtails, and guppies than about any other species, with the result that strains have been established in some of them for the early recognition of sex in the newly dropped young. This is done by color linkage; thus, before the gonopodium develops, it is still possible to tell the males from the females, all of one sex being of a particular color or spotted with black.

**FERTILIZATION**

Young live-bearing females can be fertilized at a very early stage (in the case of platies, some eight days or so after birth) if mature males are present. Otherwise, they must wait for their brothers to attain maturity, which will delay fertilization considerably. Even when fertilized very early, the females do not bear young for many weeks and may be expected to drop their first brood not earlier than 10 to 12 weeks in the case of guppies, platies, and swordtails, and then only if kept quite warm (26° to 27 °C). The act of insemination is very rapid and frequent; males take no notice of whether a female is already gravid or even about to drop young but pay court to all and sundry, including immature males. They typically hover around the female or chase her about the tank, often with a spreading of fins and, particularly in the swordtails, with a backward swimming motion which is very characteristic. The female seems indifferent to all this, and the male appears to dart in and eject his sperm when the chance presents itself. However, it is thought that the female has in fact to cooperate if the sperm are to enter her reproductive tract. The sperm are stored in the female and fertilize successive crops of egg cells for the next five or six months. If fertilization continues to occur, as, of course, it does in a mixed tank, the new sperm certainly fertilize some of the eggs, but the extent to which the first, original insemination can be superseded by later ones has never been fully worked out.

In the guppy, the platy, the swordtail, the mollie, and gambusia, successive crops of eggs are fertilized at discrete intervals, so that one lot of young, all the same age, is produced, followed about a month later by another batch. At an average temperature of about 24 °C, the actual development of the young from the time of fertilization to birth is about 24 days, and the brood interval is about 30 days. The extra week is taken up by the development of the next crop of eggs prior to their actually being fertilized.

In *Heterandria* and *Poeciliopsis* and some of their relatives, the eggs ripen and are fertilized at much more frequent intervals, batches being produced every few days and young being born at similar intervals, so that there are always young at different stages present in the mother and a few are dropped at a time.

## DEVELOPMENT

Most live-bearers produce young at about 22-day intervals at about 27 °C and in a bright light. At 20 °C and still in a bright light, the interval lengthens to some 35 days or more. In a dull light it also lengthens, and, as remarked above, cool conditions plus dullness will stop reproduction.

During development the young fishes are nourished by their mother. They do not simply lie in her body protected from harm and dependent on the yolk in the egg; instead, there are various devices in different species by which they receive nourishment just as do the young of a mammal. All the same, they do have a yolk sac (the bag containing nourishment which is present in the egg when fertilization takes place) and continue to use up the food stored within it. The maternal nourishment is typically provided by a *placenta*, an organ in which the blood of the mother and that of the young are very closely mingled without actual mixing, and which is remarkable in that it is part of the pericardium or membrane surrounding the heart itself. The young fishes develop in a folded position, head to tail, and are born with this fold still present. At birth they may sink to the bottom for a short period, but they are usually able to fend for themselves immediately. They are quite variable in size, according to the age of their mother and their own numbers; large broods often contain young fishes half the size of those in smaller broods. An average length for the newly born swordtail or platy is about 6 mm. The first brood from a young female may number only 6; later broods may rise to 200. Mollies, however, rarely exceed 30 or 40, and a typical swordtail, guppy, or platy brood is 60 to 80.

In most live-bearers, the pregnant mother swells unmistakably and also presents the well-known "gravid spot," which is a dark spot near the base of the anal fin caused by the stretching of the peritoneal wall. Some of the hybrid swordtail varieties, particularly those of low fertility, can catch us unawares by not showing these signs very clearly and by giving birth to an unexpected batch of 20 or 30 young. Moving the mother is apt to cause premature birth, particularly in mollies; she is best moved early or very late, so that the young either are in no danger or are so nearly ready for birth that they come to no harm. Many fanciers avoid moving mollies more than is absolutely necessary and would prefer to lose a fair proportion of the young rather than disturb the adult females too frequently. Caesarian section has been successfully performed with several species.

At birth, the young swim towards the light (positive phototropism). If the tank is heavily stocked with fine-leaved plants, particularly towards the lightest side or end, they will migrate into them and be fairly safe from the adults or from their mother; they may otherwise all be eaten. Curiously enough, the young live-bearer stands a better chance of surviving in a crowded tank with mixed sizes of fish of the same species than it does if only its mother or a few adults are present. Why this is so is not known.

## SAVING THE YOUNG

Various traps have been designed for the relatively rapid

separation of the young from their mother at birth. They are improvements on an old idea, which was to place the mother in a funnel in a jar. Although she could not swim through the small hole, the young could escape and survive. Such a restricted arrangement does not suit many females, and it is more frequently the practice to use a small aquarium with a cage suspended in it having walls of such material that the young can escape.

Perforated metal is to be avoided, but plastic is safe. A cage or barrier of glass rods is satisfactory but tedious to make and rather expensive to buy. Perhaps the most satisfactory arrangement is a screen of mosquito netting on a stainless steel or wooden frame, which can be wedged across the tank so as to confine the female to one end while allowing the young to pass. Even a loose-fitting dividing glass is fairly good, as the young seem to find the slots at the edges quite rapidly and make their way past.

Despite all these devices, most breeders prefer the more natural method of having plants in abundance to provide shelter for the young and removing the mother at the earliest chance. Moving the young is not to be recommended at so early a stage. If the mother is supplied with more live food than she can eat, she is unlikely to destroy many of her own young; hence the addition of mosquito larvae or *Daphnia*. If the young have to be moved, do not use a net. Either siphon them off as gently as possible or, better still, ladle them out with a soup ladle or teacup. Mollies will usually not eat their young unless they are hungry, so if this species is well-fed young will be present in plenty without further precautions. The best plants for young live-bearers are masses of *Myriophyllum, Ambulia, Nitella, Utricularia* (bladderwort), or even algae. They allow the young to dive in for protection but are too dense for the adult to follow with any ease.

Young born prematurely may still have a visible bulge formed by the yolksac and will be small. They are often poor swimmers and are likely to die off rapidly. Sometimes the addition of a little salt to the water helps, about a quarter teaspoon to the liter, making roughly a 0.1% solution, or even more. Young mollies or guppies are quite happy in a 1% salt solution; if bred from marine-acclimatized parents, they can take a 3% solution.

# FEEDING THE YOUNG

Live-bearer young are quite large as young fishes go and can be fed dry or other prepared food straight away. If they are given only prepared food, growth will be poor, but a mixture of live and dry food is quite satisfactory. The influence of a few feedings of young *Daphnia* on the subsequent growth rate of newly dropped platies is quite remarkable, and this early feeding of live food is very important for good development. Later it matters much less, although the fishes will still do better with a good proportion of live foods.

They should be fed several times daily and kept at not lower than 24 °C. Young fishes can take high temperatures and thrive in them and they do not like cool water permanently, although they can take chills remarkably well. They like to keep their bellies full and should go around looking like fishes stuck onto a small football for the first few weeks. They will not overeat, no matter how they look. If much dry food is used, and of course it must be suitably small in size, scavengers should be present. Snails are the easiest to install, but *Corydoras* will not eat the young fishes as long as there are left-overs to clear up.

Suitable first live foods are microworms, newly hatched brine shrimp, shredded earthworm, sifted *Daphnia*, newly hatched mosquito wrigglers or shredded white worms. Sifted *Daphnia* are those which have been passed through a fine mesh, eliminating the adults or near-adults. Actually, if adult *Daphnia* are used in reasonable numbers—so as not to overcrowd the tank and compete seriously for oxygen—their young are a continual source of food. Suitable dry foods include any fine powder food, such as dried shrimp finely ground, fine cereals, liver or egg powder, and various commercial preparations.

These can be followed a week or so later by larger live foods and coarser dry foods, although the smaller sizes will still be eaten. To the diet may be added tubifex worms, larger larvae of various species, and adult *Daphnia*.

It is believed by many that it is particularly important to feed mollies little and often, although no critical experiments have been reported on this point. The young should therefore be fed up to six or eight times a day, if possible, and a comparison made with the effects of the same amount of food given, say, twice a day to another batch from the same brood. Only such experiments can settle these questions, but to be of value they must be carefully made on identical batches of fish housed exactly alike, so that effects of the feeding regime can be identified with reasonable certainty and not be confused with other variables.

## STRAINS

The platys, swordtails, and mollies exist in many varieties, and the first two cross readily, so readily that it is doubtful whether the great majority of so-called platys and swords are in fact pure. Most of them are hybrids of one type or another.

Some of the hereditary factors (genes) concerned in the size, color, or configuration of these fishes have been studied in detail, while others have not. Some characteristics are clear-cut, present or absent, whereas others are the result of the combined action of several genes and exist in all sorts of grades and shades. Thus, red and green in the swordtail are mutually incompatible colors—a fish is either red or it is green, and both may be produced by the same parents. Moreover, the redness of the red or the greenness of the green are not affected by the fact that they have come from a parent of another color, although the intensity *may* be affected by other factors, some genetic and some environmental. Thus it *may* be true that a really good red swordtail can be bred only from red stock, because only then could factors tending to intensify the redness be properly concentrated and observed. However, this is all conjecture, and observation on the point is needed.

A good practical example is the wagtail platy. This fish carries two factors which together produce the black tail and fins characteristic of its type. Whenever these two factors come together in any sort of platy, wagtail must result. The factors are that producing the "comet" appearance, and another, "E," which shows no visible effect on its own, but which, when present with comet, causes wagtail. American wagtails, the home of origin of the strain, have a considerable amount of black on the fleshy part of the tail as well as on the finny part. This is regarded as undesirable by British aquarists, who have succeeded in altering the appearance of wagtails by selective breeding so that many of

191

the modified stock have no black on the base of the fin. This was achieved by selecting genes that affect the actions of the two "main genes" which must be present for wagtail to show at all. Clearly, these genes with small modifying effects could be selected only in the presence of the wagtail feature itself, and thus the particular British standard wagtail *must* be bred from wagtail stock.

In general, therefore, really fine specimens and really worthwhile strains, whether for color or other features, should be kept separate. The fishes do not distinguish between such differences, and any platy will mate with any other platy of opposite sex, as will males of the other species with any female of their own kind.


## HYBRIDS

Platys and swordtails hybridize readily, and some hybrids are fertile. Other species, such as the molly and the guppy, do not produce hybrids nearly so readily. Thus it is with platy-swordtail crosses that the aquarist is mainly concerned.

When placed with a mixture of platys and swords, a fish tends to mate only with its own kind, but, if it has no choice, it will mate with the other species. Thus, for hybridizing, it is best to place a mature male of one species with developing young of the other, whereupon the females will be impregnated by the adult male before their brothers have a chance to catch up. Naturally, these young males are removed as they mature, for they will interfere with the crossing later on if left around.

First-cross hybrids of the platy-swordtail varieties are large, fine-looking fishes. They usually grow bigger than either parent, exhibiting a phenomenon called "hybrid vigor." They are much more uniform than later generations, and, if they come from a mating of fairly pure lines of parents, they will be very uniform indeed. They are deep bodied, with short swords in the males. When mated back to either parent stock, fish of any desired degree of platy or swordtail "blood" can be produced. The process has been very extensively employed, sometimes by accident, in preparing aquarium varieties of the two species, and it is now suggested that they not be differentiated for classification purposes.

192

## BREEDING OUTSIDE

In temperate zones, many of the live-bearers can be bred in summer in garden pools. The mollies are particularly suited to this and produce extra-fine specimens as long as the water is reasonably warm. In a good pool, they will survive at 15 °C quite comfortably but will not breed unless at about 18° to 21 °C. It is a custom in Australia to place mollies out in the Spring and to net out the proceeds in the Fall. A small pool of some 2,000 liters will yield 1,000 young from a stocking which contained perhaps ten adults six months previously. It must be protected from predators like birds and even cats, but smaller enemies such as insect larvae fail to keep up with the molly production line.

Swordtails, platys, and guppies can be bred similarly but do not take a chill as readily as the molly (except *Xiphophorus variatus*, which can go down to 10 °C). However, there is not the need for outdoor breeding as with the molly, which produces better fishes when pondbred. It is even alleged that sailfin mollies produce a worthwhile crop of sailfin young only when bred out of doors, but of this the author has no first-hand experience.

To an extent, all the tropicals can be acclimatized to lower temperatures outside than they can stand inside, but they must not be suddenly subjected to them. When the fishes are brought in again, any necessary rise must be gradual, and the best plan is to use water from the pond in which the fishes have been kept, gradually replacing it with other water, if desired.

## CULLING LIVE-BEARER YOUNG

If live-bearers are being bred for particular qualities and colors, they must be separated very early from potential sources of crossbreeding. The scheme will vary according to circumstances, but, if an adult male of the desired type is not placed with the young so as to catch the females early, they must be segregated as soon as it is possible to tell sex and a careful watch kept for the development of male characters in their supposed sisters. By this method, the stock can be housed in two tanks, one with males and the other with females and undeveloped males, with *vigilance* as the password!

As soon as the young of the best quality can be selected, which should be possible within two months, the rest are discarded and appropriate matings are made. It is best to keep several goodlooking pairs and to progeny-test them—i.e., keep them and their offspring until you can see which lines of fishes you want, and then go on breeding from the parents, discarding the others of the same generation. Sometimes, the best parents are not the best lookers, and a fine strain of fishes may have grandparents of only second-rate appearance.

An alternative but space-consuming method used by some is to pair off all reasonable looking fishes in small receptacles, ignoring sex until you can see which are which, and then to keep moving pairs around if it becomes clear that certain jars contain two of the same sex, and also culling. By this method, all progeny can be used, if desired, yet it can be guaranteed that each female has been paired with a specific, known male. Apart from laboratory and genetic studies, the utility of this procedure is not obvious. Usually, only the best 10 to 20% of a brood is worth serious consideration for further stock improvement; why then go on breeding from inferior stock? The great advantage of fish breeding is that we can cull so drastically, using only one fish in a hundred if we wish, and yet can rapidly expand the new stock and again select vigorously for only the best.

## FORCED GROWTH

Rapid growth is generally best, producing vigorous, well-proportioned young. Excessively rapid growth is inadvisable, as the fishes often do badly and even die when placed on a more normal diet and perhaps in less favorable conditions.

It is therefore advisable to give plenty of room and food (especially live food) and to keep the tank warm and clean. Keep the young fishes in as large a tank as possible and give them plenty of room, allowing at least the air surface recommended earlier in this book. Feed often and use aeration if there is any suspicion of overcrowding; if much dry food is used, place snails in the tank and pay strict attention to cleanliness. Remember that a few good feeds of live food *early* in development are more important than they are later on. However restricted your live food supply may be, do not stint the young live-bearers for the first few days.

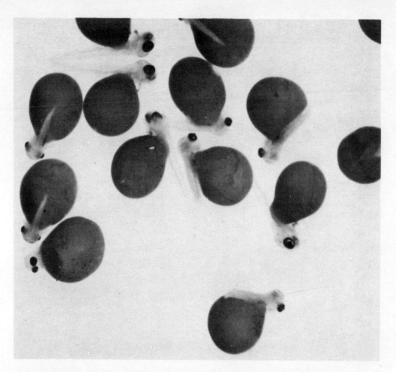

Fry retrieved from the mouth cavity of *Labeotropheus fuelleborni,* a mouth-brooding cichlid from Lake Malawi, Africa. After about 20 days of incubation, the yolk is exhausted and they leave their parent's mouth to feed by themselves.

On the other hand, even with live-bearers, which will take dry food so readily, do not feed exclusively on live food unless you are virtually sure that there will always be plenty available to them. Accustom them to some dry food even though there is ample live food, or they may suffer a bad set-back if a switch-over becomes necessary. This is particularly important if your young fishes are to pass into strange hands.

Increased length of illumination daily will keep the fishes eating longer, as long as food is supplied, but once again some regard must be paid to likely future conditions. Any great change may cause harm; therefore, if you have been forcing growth to any marked extent, slow down the pace for a week or so before the fishes are due for a change, especially if they are going to be shipped elsewhere.

195

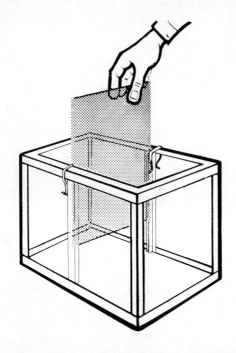

**Left:** A tank divider is a very useful device for isolating parents from each other or from their spawn. An over-aggressive male can harm a non-receptive female, and most fishes eat their own spawn. **Below:** To a limited extent, egg predation can be reduced by having fine-leaved plants in the breeding tank of egg scatterers, like the common tetra *Hyphessobrycon flammeus.*

# CHAPTER TEN

## Breeding the Egg Scatterers

Most of the egg-laying fishes are quite a different proposition from the live-bearers when it comes to breeding. They are a more immediate nuisance but ultimately less trouble. That is to say, induction of spawning and coping with it needs more preparation as does feeding and raising the young, but, when all that is over, the adults can be kept in communities and will generally only spawn to order.

The egg scatterers include most aquarium fishes—the Characidae, the Cyprinidae, and the Cyprinodontidae. Most, like the goldfish, lay adhesive eggs which stick to plants, but some, like the zebra fish, lay non-adhesive eggs which fall to the bottom. Many eat their eggs if given the chance. The typical spawning movement is a chase of the female by the male, accompanied by spasms of egg-laying and simultaneous sperm ejection and fertilization. Activity may continue for an hour or for several days, but a few hours is the general rule.

Once live-bearer young have been produced and saved from parental cannibalism, the battle is practically over. Once the eggs of an egg-laying fish have been deposited, and this may be no mean accomplishment, the battle has just begun. The eggs must be preserved from predators and disease, they must hatch, and the young must then be protected, fed and raised. Feeding may be the worst problem, but predators run a close second. Thus, although a successful spawning and raising of an egg-laying species *may* occur in an unprepared tank, it usually does not. It is all a question of percentage of successes. Many methods for the spawning and raising of different species are described in the literature, and the most that can be said for the majority of them is that Mr. A did succeed (usually on one occasion only) in breeding species X by such and such a method. No one (with the exception, perhaps, of a few professionals) knows how often this method will succeed or how good it is compared with the method of Mr. B, which also succeeded once or twice.

It is therefore necessary, especially with the egg scatterers, to list a number of general principles which are pretty clearly established, to indicate how improvements may be made in the future, and above all to recommend an experimental approach. Perhaps the best general advice is that few species are actually as particular about conditions for successful spawning as most people think, and that cleanliness, healthy fish, and proper feeding are usually more important than fussing about with pH, temperature, light, shade, and so forth. (Note the word "usually"— exceptions occur.)

## SEX IN EGG SCATTERERS

The majority of egg scatterers have distinguishable sexes, even out of the breeding time, and nearly all can be told apart quite easily when the female fills with roe. The standard books on fish varieties should be consulted for details of the various ways in which sex can be told. Where these do not help, it pays to remember that the male is often the slimmer and rather smaller fish and brighter colored. In the Characidae he usually has minute hooks on the lower part of the anal fin. These may sometimes be seen as a marking on the fin, or they may actually catch in a fine net and be quite a nuisance. In the Cyprinidae, the breeding males often develop small white pearly dots on some part (as on the gill covers of goldfish). Most of the barbs show color differences between the sexes, and they are very easy to sex for that reason. In the Cyprinodontidae, color differences are again the rule, which facilitates matters for the tyro provided some of each sex are present.

Determining sex early and out of the breeding time or before maturity is of course important when selecting fishes for future spawning. With practice, it is surprising how easy it is to sex a species which would baffle an amateur even when he knows what to look for.

## CLEANING TANKS

Tanks for spawning egg scatterers must usually be clean, preferably newly washed out and disinfected, but at least cleared

198

of all muck, snails, leeches, hydra, and so forth. It is virtually impossible to do this without a thorough cleaning. It is very difficult to clean and disinfect a planted tank without removing plants and gravel, unless one risks killing the plants; it is best to use unplanted spawning vessels. The fishes don't mind. They don't appreciate the beauty of a well set-up tank with rocks and gravel and plants and are just as ready to spawn in a bare tank with a little plant or spawning material anchored in an appropriate spot to receive the eggs. In fact, many will spawn in a completely bare tank, but they are much too likely to eat their eggs under these conditions. The outstanding exception to this rule is the majority of members of the Cyprinodontidae or killifishes, which are dealt with separately below.

As remarked above, many spawnings are brought through in planted, relatively dirty aquaria, for many enthusiasts actually advocate the presence of plenty of infusoria-producing material. What really matters are the chances of success and the proportion of eggs hatched and of young likely to be raised. One method may work once in three times and produce an average of 30 fishes a time—another will work two times out of three and produce 200 fishes a time (hence it is more than ten times as good a method). The clean method with washed tanks is good, although no one has yet published comparative figures to prove statistically just *how* good it is.

The tank may be washed with warm water at about 50 °C, care being taken not to crack heavy or plate glass. The water is best introduced gradually in order to displace existing water and to raise the temperature fairly slowly. Small tanks with thin glass can be treated much less carefully. The warm water should come well up under the top rim, so as to catch hidden pests. The water at 50 °C is left to cool of its own accord; dead snails, leeches, hydra, etc., are then siphoned off, and the volume is made up with tap water. Alternatively, the tank may be emptied and washed out or thoroughly rinsed with sea water or with 3 to 6% salt solution. This kills off most pests in a minute or two, as long as operculum-possessing snails are not present. The tank may even be very thoroughly washed and scrubbed with cold water. Drying a tank for a few days is not a good method, for many pests or their eggs may survive.

Plants may be cleaned by a thorough washing under a brisk cold tap, followed by a 15-second dunk in sea water or 3% salt solution and then a further brisk wash in cold water. They can be placed in water at 40 °C and left, but this will not kill all parasites and higher temperatures may kill the plants; 50 °C will certainly kill them if left for an effective period. Instead of plants, artificial spawning media may be used that can be sterilized if necessary.

Plastic mops are the best artificial medium, and may be purchased cheaply or made from nylon wool. Green-colored mops seem to be the best. These may be sterilized with hot or boiling water and may be anchored with glass beads or floated free in the aquarium with cork rings.

It is possible to use potassium permanganate or other disinfectants for cleaning both tanks and plants, but in effective strengths they are often a nuisance and kill the plants. The concentrations of permanganate frequently advocated for use in aquaria, 4-12 mg per liter, are not effective for this purpose. Effective strengths of common disinfectants are costly and rather difficult to get rid of satisfactorily. Although the residue left in the tank may be harmless, it is likely to affect the fishes and to inhibit spawning unless an inordinate amount of washing-out is done.

## SETTING UP TANKS

Suitable tank sizes for the egg scatterers are 10 to 60 liters for tropicals, according to the size and nature of the fishes, with larger tanks for goldfish. Small, light tanks are more easily cleaned and set up than heavy ones, and since we are not concerned with cultivating infusoria in them their size matters little at the spawning stage, as long as there is room for the parent fishes to follow their particular routine. Later, the fry can be moved to a larger tank.

Most characins, small cyprinids, and cyprinodonts can be spawned in a 10-liter tank (35 cm in length). For the usual scatterers of adhesive eggs, a bunch of fine-leaved plants or algae, or one or more plastic mops are placed in about the center of the tank and weighted down with a small stone or with glass. There should be room for the fishes to swim around and over this material. Suitable plants are *Myriophyllum, Ambulia, Nitella,* and the thread-like green algae. *Anacharis* is particularly unsuitable since it dies readily after most available disinfection methods, except for plain washing.

The medium barbs, like *Puntius conchonius* or *P. ticto,* should have somewhat larger, say 20-liter, tanks otherwise similarly arranged. This size is suitable for the danios, although those that scatter non-adhesive eggs require a different set-up. Only really large fishes like the goldfish require big tanks, and it is surprising what can be done with a 40- to 60-liter tank, even with these.

A dividing glass with rubber-covered edges (as for the top of the tank when a flush cover is used) is useful for some varieties. This is used for separating the fishes before spawning is required. Adequate illumination must be provided, since many fishes like a well-lit spawning area. It is the custom of some European aquarists to use a spotlight, illuminating only an area of the tank in which the fishes will come and spawn. Tanks should also have means for controlling temperature individually as it will sometimes be necessary to raise or lower it to produce the required results.

The bottom of such a spawning tank should have a layer of about 0.5 cm of well-washed peat, which will help to condition the water or keep it conditioned and will receive any eggs which fall to the base of the tank, hiding them from the parents and helping to preserve them. Peat water, prepared as described above, is essential for really successful spawning of some fishes, particularly the characins, and never does harm to those that can get along without it. Neons (*Paracheirodon innesi*) must have very soft acid water: more than about 15 ppm hardness prevents the development of the neon egg. The cardinal tetra (*Cheirodon axelrodi*) does not require such soft water, but is otherwise to be treated the same, while other species such as glowlights (*Hemigrammus erythrozonus*) and rosy-finned tetras (*Hyphessobrycon rosaceus*) need quite soft water, although it need not be as soft as for neons. The combination of plastic mops, very soft and acid peat-soaked water of pH 6.0 to 6.5, and peat itself on the bottom of the tank is the key to successful handling of the "problem" tetras, as of that of many other species.

Peat (or peat moss) absorbs quite a variety of toxic substances, and, in addition, it takes up potassium, calcium and magnesium and softens and acidifies the water, acting like a rather weak ion-exchange resin. It may also contain antibiotic substances which may play a role in suppressing bacterial growth and thus preserve the eggs. Certainly, eggs in peat water develop better, fungus less often and die less often than in ordinary water, soft or otherwise. Since a sudden change to the adult fishes must be avoided, they may need to be acclimatized to the new conditions before spawning if they are kept in an ordinary community tank, but the need for this varies. Some fishes, particularly some of the characins, can be killed by a transfer from medium hard water to soft peat water.

## SPAWNING

If the fishes are kept at an average temperature of 24 °C, the majority will spawn without a rise in temperature. All that is necessary is to place a ripe pair into the spawning tank with as little disturbance as possible. Exceptions to this rule are few; these include *Hyphessobrycon pulchripinnis* (lemon tetra), *Neolebias* species, *Brachydanio nigrofasciatus, Rasbora heteromorpha,* and some of the barbs, notably *Barbodes everetti, Puntius nigrofasciatus,* and *Capoeta tetrazona.* All these are said to do better if the temperature is raised to about 27 °C. On the other hand there is good evidence that *Rasbora trilineata* and *Tanichthys albonubes* spawn well at 21 °C and that the latter does not like a higher temperature. The common goldfish (*Carassius auratus*) spawns at about 21 °C. and, in common with a few other species, may be stimulated to spawn by a slight *fall* in temperature. Many of these fishes will spawn at lower temperatures in open pools.

The pair of fish placed in the breeding tank must be ready to spawn. For this, they are best conditioned for a week or so before with live food, although many species do not always require this procedure. The female should be full of spawn, bulging, but not left too long, or the eggs may not be fertile and she may become egg-bound and die. A thin female will sometimes spawn, but usually she gives few eggs; if she has a normal quota, she will not be thin. The male should look pert and well-colored. He may pale off on being moved, but he should rapidly regain his form, even within a few minutes. Young males may not fertilize all the eggs and young females will not give a very large number of eggs, but there is no other reason why they should not be spawned. Keeping fishes for two years before spawning, when they are ready at six months, is pure waste and may create the many difficulties that occur when they are spawned later. Fish should spawn early and spawn regularly for the best results. Often, a female will be ready every 10 to 14 days and a male twice as frequently. Do not chase the prospective breeding pair all over their tank to catch them and then expect them to spawn immediately. They will be too scared in most cases.

The fish may spawn immediately, or they may wait several days, but somebody must be ready at frequent intervals to inspect the tank and remove the fish if they have spawned. It is best to watch the whole process and take them out as soon as spawning is over, since they must be removed immediately or there may be few eggs uneaten. Even flooding the tank with live food does not always prevent egg eating, although it may help. Food should not be given during spawning, for it may terminate the process.

If fish do not spawn quickly, they may do so early the next morning; therefore be up within two hours of dawn or cover the tank so that it will stay dark and daylight may be admitted at your convenience. Alternatively, place the glass divider in position with one fish on each side of it and let them contemplate each other for a spell. This often helps so much that some breeders use the device regularly for a few hours or days before allowing the pair to come together. It is unnecessary in most instances, however. With some of the barbs, frequent partial changes of fresh tap water may induce spawning. These do not require soft and acid water and so may be subjected to this procedure.

If the fish have not spawned within two days, gradually raise the temperature by 2° to 3°C. This often stimulates spawning quite promptly, but wait for another day or so if nothing happens. If spawning has still not occurred after three or four days, it is usually best to remove the pair, separate them, or place them in a large community tank and try again a few days later. If they are kept in the spawning tank for more than two days, they should be given live food in moderation.

Variations on the above procedure include the routine placing of breeders in the tank after dark to induce spawning the next morning, placing the female in about half a day ahead of the male, and placing two males with one female in the case of many characins and the danios. This is thought to increase the percentage of fertilized eggs, but it is a rather hazardous procedure in many cases, as the males seem to spend more time chasing each other than chasing the female.

The spawning action varies with the species. Most of them indulge in the typical chase of the female by the male, but some start with the reverse procedure, and the female chases the male. This is often seen in *Hemigrammus ocellifer* (head and tail light tetra) and in *Capoeta tetrazona* (Sumatra barb). Finally, however, it is the male who chases. He takes up a position beside the female and in or over the plant mass; with a quivering motion, the eggs and milt are released. Some species have spectacular habits at the moment of spawning. The glowlight tetra (*Hemigrammus erythrozonus*) pair does a complete barrel-roll, the giant danio (*Danio aequipinnatus*) female whirls around several times in a horizontal plane, the female *Rasbora heteromorpha* loops the loop vertically, depositing eggs on the underside of plants as she does so. In this species, as in many others, the male curls his body around the female and releases the milt as she spawns.

## KILLIFISHES

The killifishes, or Cyprinodontidae, usually produce rather large eggs which may take a considerable time to develop. The egg membrane is often very tough and the egg can be handled quite roughly without coming to harm. Sometimes the egg has projections from it which help it to cling to plants. Some species lay eggs which hatch within about a week, and the general run of *Epiplatys* varieties and some of the *Aphyosemion* take 10-14 days. Others, such as various *Nothobranchius* and *Cynolebias* species may take three to six months or longer. Moreover, some of the long-hatching eggs will never hatch at all if they are kept in water for the whole of the period concerned, but must be dried and wetted again, sometimes repeatedly, before they will do so. Some eggs develop so-called "resting fry," which are fully mature but do not hatch out; others remain as "resting eggs," which do not even develop unless drying-up and rewetting occur. However, even in those species such as the *Aphyosemions* which usually do not need a drying-out stage, this procedure results in improved culture methods because it has been found that all eggs in a batch laid over a period may be brought artificially to the same stage of development, the resting fry, by being dried out just prior to the expected first hatchings. Those eggs which were ready stay as they are, while the others catch up. This is particularly true of all bottom-spawners, which normally lay eggs in mud or, in the aquarium, in peat waiting to receive them. Even some species such as *Aphyosemion australe* (the lyretail) which usually lays eggs on plants and will do so on nylon mops, will spawn into peat if offered no alternative, and its eggs may then be processed as below.

It is, therefore, becoming the practice to spawn the killies, other than *Epiplatys, Aplocheilus,* some *Aphyosemion* and a few others, by placing a pair or a trio, or even several of each sex, into a peat-lined tank and allowing spawning to occur over a period at fairly low temperatures—from 20° to 24°C, depending on the usual length of time the eggs take to hatch. At the end of this time, or earlier if desired, the fish are removed and the peat is lifted from the tank with a very fine net. It is squeezed lightly in the hand and placed in a shallow dish to dry out, in a warm, but not hot, situation. When the peat is fairly dry, like moist tobacco, the eggs are easily seen and may be examined under a lens or microscope. When it is somewhat drier, but not quite dry and crumbly, it may be placed in an air-tight container or plastic bag and stored for a period before hatching. This period varies with species; most *Aphyosemion* will stand a week or two, but *Cynolebias* species will keep for many months. For hatching, the peat should be placed in soft water, preferably peat water, and a little fine dry food added, which seems to help matters, perhaps by promoting bacterial action in assisting softening of the egg membranes. Hatching of many eggs should occur simultaneously, but some may require a further period of drying before they will do so.

The other "panchax-like" varieties may be allowed to spawn

A pair of harlequin rasboras, *Rasbora heteromorpha*, spawning on the undersurface of a broad leaf.

The ventral fins of the female *Corydoras* often serve as a carrying pouch for the eggs that are then attached to a suitable substrate, like the leaves and stems of plants or any other surface in the tank.

**Right:** The "splashing tetra," *Copella arnoldi,* gets its common name from its unusual spawning behavior; as seen here, the breeding pair actually leave the water to spawn on a leaf exposed outside the tank.
**Below:** The breeding tank for the common angelfish, *Pterophyllum scalare,* should be provided with some type of substrate, like broad-leaved plants, a piece of slate or ceramic flowerpots.

onto plants or mops suspended in the water, which may be removed at intervals for the fry to be hatched in another tank, so as to avoid being eaten by their parents. It is frequently advised that salt be added to the water, but this is rarely of use. A somewhat higher temperature range is best, say 23° to 26°C. The eggs may be collected particularly easily from mops and may be stored in separate small receptacles with, if necessary, a little methylene blue or acriflavine added as a guard against fungus, any spoiled eggs being removed daily. These eggs will hatch out over a period and the fry will need sorting from time to time to prevent cannibalism. As an alternative to moving spawning material plus eggs, the parents may be shifted from tank to tank at, say, weekly intervals. The eggs they leave behind are then allowed to hatch without disturbance.

A good female of typical fertility will lay 10-20 eggs per day for several days and then may, or may not, have a rest. If a trio is kept per tank, it may be expected that perhaps 20 eggs per day will accumulate on the average, and thus each week's spawning could give up to 140 young. This is rarely achieved, but at least several dozen should survive and hatch per week, whether collected in peat or on plants or mops. In either case, the eggs may be examined and their state of development checked quite easily with a hand lens. The "eyed" stage, when the eyes are visible as two black dots in the egg, is particularly easy to see.

## ABERRANT TYPES

The above account covers many of the egg scatterers which lay adhesive eggs. A few lay non-adhesive eggs, outstanding among which is *Brachydania rerio* (zebra fish). With this fish, and with the related fishes, *B. nigrofasciatus* and *B. albolineatus* (pearl danio), it is necessary to catch the eggs as they fall to prevent their being eaten. This may be done by coating the bottom of the tank with small marbles or pebbles, preferably interlaced with plants, with peat, or by means of a grid of glass rods or other material which will allow the eggs to fall beneath and prevent the parents from following. Fairly shallow water, not more than 15 cm, is also to be recommended, since it prevents the adults from having too long a time in which to chase and eat the falling eggs, as they tend to spawn near the surface.

*Copella arnoldi* lays adhesive spawn above the water line and should be given a sheet of sanded glass or similar material projecting several inches into the air and slanting at an angle of about 45°. The fishes leap into the air and deposit the eggs some 5 cm above the top of the water; these are guarded by the male from some distance off, and at frequent intervals he dashes over and splashes them with water.

The bloodfin (*Aphyocharax anisitsi*) may also leap out of the water when spawning, but the eggs fall back into the water and, being non-adhesive, sink to the bottom, as with *Brachydanio*. The croaking tetra (*Glandulocauda inequalis*) was a puzzle to breeders for a long time until it was found that a normal-appearing courtship is not followed immediately by egg laying. This occurs a day or so later, in the absence of the male, when the female deposits fertile eggs singly on the leaves of plants. This fish gets its name from the noise made by males.

A number of fishes are community breeders, spawning in large groups of mixed sexes. This happens with some of the barbs, such as *Puntius conchonius* and *P. ticto*, but they are also able to spawn in pairs. Some of the *Rasbora* are much more choosy and very rarely spawn except in communities. *Rasbora heteromorpha* will spawn fairly readily when at least 8 to 12 fish are present and very readily in communities of larger size, when unfortunately the eggs are nearly all consumed on the spot by the onlookers. The best results so far have been reported with smaller groups placed in planted tanks so that their habit of depositing eggs on the underside of growing plants can be practiced. Breeders are removed as soon as activity ceases or as soon as any of the fish present begin to eat the eggs. *Rasbora heteromorpha* may also spawn side-by-side over rooted plants as do many other species. What determines the particular behavior pattern adopted is unknown.

Goldfish spawn with a grand chase in true carp fashion but have no special requirements except reasonable space. The hardier varieties will spawn at 15° to 18°C or even lower, but the fancy types are said to need 20°C or thereabouts. They need more plants on which to spawn than do most tropicals, and again two males to a female are often advocated.

# INCUBATION OF THE EGGS

The great majority of fish eggs hatch in one day or less at 24° to 27 °C. It is best to keep the temperature at the same level as when spawning occurred; however, fish eggs can stand fluctuations quite well, but in this case *downward* better than upward. The same is true of young fry. There are many reports of characin eggs taking two or three days to hatch, and, although some are undoubtedly correct, it still remains true that the majority of young are hatched within the first day. They are often difficult to see, and it may be two or three days before they hang on the glass or on plants and become easier to find; thus, it is easy to get the impression that they have not hatched out for longer than is the case. Most barbs are out by 24 to 36 hours, taking perhaps a little longer than the typical characin. *Brachydanio* take about three days, as does *Copella arnoldi* and some of the pencilfishes (*Nannostomus*). Cyprinodonts usually take much longer, as noted above.

At lower temperatures, most eggs take longer to hatch, and, since they will survive better than the fishes would, it is possible to ship fish eggs without elaborate precautions. Little use has been made of this procedure so far, and numerous snags will no doubt emerge when it is attempted on any scale, but the fascinating possibility remains that in the not very distant future the plastic bag may be replaced by a small vial of fertile eggs or of deep-frozen live embryos! Shipping of cyprinodont eggs is common, either dried in peat or in small containers.

After spawning is completed, eggs should be sought in the tank. They may be attached to weeds or appear like very small glass beads on the bottom. They should remain clear, and the development of the embryo should be watched to check that all is well. Infertile eggs quickly become opaque and fungused, looking like powder-puffs, with white filaments of fungus sprouting in all directions. Fertile eggs lying next to a mass of fungus-covered infertiles may be attacked, but they usually remain unaffected. It is tedious but not impossible to pipette off the fungused eggs. However, it is not really necessary in most instances.

If you cannot see the eggs, don't despair, as they are hard to spot until you are used to it, and sometimes even then. Once you have observed those of a particular species, it will be much easier to see them the next time.

## HATCHING

When the eggs hatch, the young fry still have a yolk sac, containing the remains of the nourishment of the egg. On this they live for a short time, sometimes only one or two days, sometimes as long as five days, before taking other food. For the first half day or day they often remain quietly at the bottom of the tank in the mulm or plants. In some species they take flea-like hops up into the water, sinking back again afterwards. In practically all species they then attach themselves to the glass or to plants or both, hanging motionless for an additional one or two days, still not feeding. They may also hang under the surface film of the water, and they frequently start on the glass and then transfer to the surface film. Finally the yolk sac is absorbed and they swim freely in the water, hugging the bottom or plant clumps in daylight and spreading all over the tank at night or in the dark.

At the stage when the fry cling to the glass, it is easy to see them in the right light, which is preferably from behind or the side. They cling head-upward and each is visible as a little glass splinter with a fat tummy (the yolk sac) and two very large eyes. Watch the yolk sac go down, for when it does, the time to feed is near. In the later free-swimming stage they are less easily seen, and the best time is at night. Use a flashlight or a hand-lamp of some kind and send a gentle beam across the tank from one side; the fry will be seen swimming in midwater. They may be counted with fair accuracy at this stage or at the clinging stage before it. The best way to count is to choose a typical section of the tank and count it carefully, then multiply by the figure representing the relative size of the section to the tank as a whole. It is good practice to make this count, so as to check what is happening later on and to estimate food requirements. With practice, a good look at the tank of fry will enable you to guess with sufficient accuracy to within 25 to 30%.

A pair of blue acaras, *Aequidens pulcher,* engaged in a pre-spawning ritual of a seemingly aggressive nature which, however, rarely causes injury, except when one of the fish is considerably bigger or extremely aggressive.

A female South African mouthbrooder, *Pseudocrenilabrus philander,* surrounded by free-swimming fry. During the short fry-guarding stage, the fry can seek refuge in her mouth cavity when exposed to danger.

# CHAPTER ELEVEN

## Breeding the Anabantids, Cichlids, and Some Others

Anabantid and cichlid fishes take care of their eggs and young. The extent of this care differs with different species and is most fully developed in the cichlids, which provide instances of most fascinating parental solicitude and painstaking supervision of affairs. Linked with this development is a strong tendency to a savage disposition toward other fishes in general or to others of the same species. The former is seen most in the cichlids and the latter in the anabantids, with the famous Siamese fighting fish (*Betta splendens*) as an outstanding example.

The anabantids are bubblenest builders, the male usually producing the nest and guarding the young on his own. The eggs float in the mass of bubbles until they hatch, and the fry remain in the nest for some time after this. The male is usually fierce at this stage and may kill the female if she remains in the tank. The cichlids are more cooperative, both parents taking care of the eggs and young, which are usually placed in depressions in the gravel on rocks, or on the leaves of plants. The eggs are fanned, mouthed about, and even moved from place to place, and the young are shepherded around in a flock with watchful, savage parents on guard all the time.

### SEX DIFFERENCES

Most species of the two families have well-marked sex differences in the fully adult fish, but some are very difficult to tell, in particular the angelfish (*Pterophyllum scalare*) and Discus species. Apart from frequent color differences, the males tend to have longer and more pointed dorsal and anal fins and are more brilliant, even out of the breeding season, when they are magnificent. An anabantid female full of roe is usually very plump, but cichlids may show little or nothing.

As he begins to feel ready for breeding, the male anabantid starts to blow bubbles, sticky with secretion, at the surface of the water. It is easy to see how this has evolved from the habit of these labyrinth fishes of breathing air at the surface and why surface nests are an advantage in the foul water their air-breathing habits enable them to inhabit. The chosen site is often under a leaf of a floating plant or at the edge of a mass of duckweed or algae. When the bubblenest is seen, it is time to find a ripe female and prepare for spawning.

The cichlids like to choose their mates and may kill one judged to be unsuitable. It is therefore best to use the group system, in which young fish are kept together until some pair off and can be separated for breeding. This process is apt to involve casualties, but so is any method with these bloodthirsty fellows. Another method is to introduce pairs to each other and watch. If all goes well, so much the better, but if it does not, be prepared to remove one of the pair before it is injured or even killed. The loser is not always the female.

## SUITABLE TANKS

Since the parents take the place of the aquarist and guard the eggs, there is no need for disinfected or bare tanks, although snails, planaria, and so forth are best avoided. In fact, since the fry of anabantids are small and need the finest microscopic food at the start, they are best supplied with this by the mulm and decaying material in the spawning tank, although it is not actually very difficult to make up the deficiency if a clean tank is used. The cichlids do not need such fine food, since their young are quite large; hence their tank can be clean or dirty, just as you please, for the parents will keep the eggs spotless. If, however, you wish to hatch out cichlid eggs in the absence of the parents, they must be removed to a very clean tank and particular care taken of them.

Both families should have large tanks for spawning, the anabantids because they are in need of infusorial food in plenty, and the cichlids because they are usually big fishes. For the anabantids, the tank should be well-planted and not too deep, up to 25 cm at most, and preferably tightly covered to protect the surface nest. Most cichlids tear up plants at mating time, so it is a little superfluous to have them present, but it doesn't matter to the fishes. Both like a temperature around 27°C, and many species will not spawn at temperatures much below it. Even if the cichlids are given no plants, there should be a good layer of gravel, as this is used in nest-making.

## ANABANTID COURTSHIP AND SPAWNING

Not only do the anabantids and cichlids take care of the young, but they are also more demonstrative beforehand. In fact, these are the highest developed fishes in this respect, with several quite endearing traits.

When his nest is ready, spreading a few inches across the water and with a central depth of perhaps half an inch for a big fish, the anabantid male looks around for the female. He is ambivalent in his attitude to her and is unfortunately quite likely to attack her instead of mating. The male betta assumes a fighting attitude, but whether he attacks depends on the attitude adopted by the female. She should respond with a submissive stance; if she doesn't she will be liable to attack. Another male normally adopts a fighting stance and so the battle is on. Look out for squalls, therefore, but don't remove the female unnecessarily. It is a matter of indifference whether the male is placed in her tank or she in his, except that it seems a pity to waste his nest if he has made a good one.

If all goes well, the male may drive the female below the nest, circling her with a display of erect fins and protuberant gill covers in the case of bettas. As they swim below the nest, the male encircles the female in an embrace in which his head meets his tail, and they sink slowly downwards, with the release of a number of eggs. These the male then dives down and catches, puffing them into the bubblenest with his mouth. Further embraces and spawning follow at intervals for perhaps several hours.

An interesting variation of the above is when the female remains in a corner of the tank and the male remains under the nest, and she dashes up at intervals without any encouragement, to indulge in the nuptial embrace. As soon as it is over, she scoots back to her corner until the next time. One is tempted to suppose that this must be an experienced lady who doesn't like being beaten up by her spouse and takes the least chance possible.

When spawning is over, the male takes complete charge and the female should be removed. He continues to blow bubbles and to restore any falling eggs to the nest, but subsequent behavior varies with species. With most, it is best to remove the male at hatching, which is about two days after spawning, for even the best of fathers is likely to start eating the young at the end of the first week. Leave him there until the eggs do hatch, however, as he performs a useful function in keeping them afloat and healthy.

## CICHLID COURTSHIP AND SPAWNING

When an established pair of cichlids are seen to be suited to each other, they may be left to their own devices, and sooner or later they will spawn. It is only when trying out new pairs that the aquarist must exercise surveillance and be ready to remove the vanquished. However, at a later stage, if spawning has taken place and anything goes wrong, or if all the young are suddenly removed, the pair are likely to quarrel, as if they suspected each other of the fell deed.

Courtship is more like a wrestling match than anything else. At first, approaches are made with spreading fins and body quivers, but soon the fishes take each other by the mouth and start a regular tussle. They roll over and over, tugging and writhing very vigorously, and woe to the one who tires unduly quickly. For this reason, some attempt at matching sizes when introducing new pairs to each other is not a bad scheme, although there are many very dissimilar-sized pairs who get along quite well.

At length, the contestants start clearing a place for the spawning, and it is given a very thorough going-over for several days. Large stones are favorite spots, but in their absence a patch of glass may be cleaned. Light objects are said to be preferred, so marble or other light-colored stone is often offered. As spawning approaches, a breeding tube appears in both sexes in front of the vent. When it first becomes visible, spawning is imminent, and within a day or two the tube lengthens to about 1 cm and spawning takes place.

The female deposits the eggs a few at a time on the prepared surface and is followed by the male who inseminates them. Often they are laid in very regular order, row upon row, until in the course of several hours up to 2,000 are deposited and fertilized. From then on, a constant guard is kept, and the eggs are frequently fanned and inspected. Opinions differ as to whether the primary function of this fanning is aeration or the prevention of disease by keeping fungus particles from settling. The former seems more likely, as fanning may in fact cause the deposition of fungus or bacteria which would otherwise not reach the eggs. In any case, the fishes also clean the eggs and eat any that become fungused.

Towards the end of the incubation period, which lasts three to four days, the parents dig pits in the gravel. Often two or three are dug, but finally it is decided to use one of them, and as the young hatch they are soon moved to it. Both parents participate in this, often alternating from spawning area to the gravel pit in lightning dashes, one transferring a mouthful of young, the other taking up the vacated position. This transfer system continues until the young are free-swimming, which may be for another three or four days. Each time they are moved to a new pit, they are mouthed over and spat into their new creche. Since the object of the move can hardly be to guard them, as the parents could presumably do this without shifting them around, it is again suggested that the process is one of cleaning. Moving the young from one pit to another is thought to ensure that every one is well mouthed and cleaned. There is no good evidence that this is necessary, and it seems best to admit that we do not know why the frequent moves are made.

While in the pits, the young live on the yolk sac and look like a mass of animated jelly, which gradually resolves into wriggling and hopping entities who finally swim up into the water. They are closely guarded and herded together into a swarm, those straying too far being sucked up and spat back into the multitude. They are quite large and should now be fed small live food. The parents will continue their vigil for weeks, and it is best to let them do so with at least a few of their young. The rest can be removed to a separate tank if desired at quite an early stage, but the sight of the parental care is well worth observing for as long as possible. It is quite fascinating to see the parents eating *Daphnia* or mosquito larvae of about the same size as their own fry, picking them out from among the young fishes, or even taking a mixed mouthful and spitting out the fry. They make few mistakes, if any, for the swarm of young does not diminish. At night, even when the young are quite big, they all settle down on the floor of the tank, and the parents sit over them like a pair of hens.

*Pterophyllum scalare*, the angelfish, lay its eggs on large plant leaves, preferably giant *Sagittaria* or *Echinodorus*. Alternatively, the pair will accept upright slate or opaque glass bars or rods, or even the aquarium glass itself. They do not dig pits but move the young from one leaf to another until they are free-swimming, at which time the parents guard them as usual. The parents are particularly likely to eat their spawn, so it is commercial practice to remove the leaf or rod on which the spawn has been deposited to a clean tank with a gentle trickle or aeration to replace the parents' fanning. It is frequently alleged that the angelfishes will spawn, or that their young will thrive, only in acid water. Although this is certainly untrue, it seems to be much easier to spawn them in most soft-water districts, where the water is usually also neutral to acid, but they will spawn plentifully at pH 7.2 or even higher, perhaps as long as the water is soft. However, this does not seem to have received critical attention. Sex in the angel is very difficult to tell; even other angels do not seem to find it too easy, as two females will pair off and lay sterile eggs.

The various types of discus behave much like *Symphysodon aequifasciata axelrodi* (the brown discus), which has now been bred in captivity many times. This fish deposits its eggs on large plant leaves, rocks or slate like the angels, but they cannot be easily reared in the absence of the parents, because the fry are dependent for the first few weeks on the production of mucus from the parents' bodies. Both sexes produce a copious slime which the young peck at for nourishment. Complicated and not always satisfactory replacements for this mucus have been developed. The discus also need soft, acid water for breeding, and a temperature of 27° to 30°C.

Some cichlids have moved a stage further in the care of their young and retain the eggs and fry in the mouth for several weeks. During this time, the parent that guards the young starves. In

*Pseudocrenilabrus multicolor* (Egyptian mouthbrooder) it is the female. The devoted parent gets very thin, and since he or she has a large head to begin with, assumes a very emaciated appearance.

The young swim out and feed, but rush back to the parent's mouth at any alarm, and learn to fend for themselves only when they get too large for all of them to get back in again.

Many of the African cichlids are mouthbrooders and despite their normal fierceness make good parents. The female is often the guardian.

The dwarf cichlids are gentler than their larger cousins and do not attack other fishes or tear up plants when breeding. The female seems sometimes to take charge of the eggs and young and even drives the male off, but without harming him.


## OTHER SPECIES

Various other aquarium fishes can be bred, some very sporadically and others with regularity. They form a miscellaneous group about which more and more is becoming known.

The *Corydoras* of various species (South American armored catfishes) breed fairly well in captivity, particularly *C. aeneus* and *C. paleatus*, or perhaps it is only that these have been most tried out. They lay eggs on plants or on the glass and do not harm either them or the young. The eggs hatch in three or four days, and the young like to disappear into a thick bed of humus or mulm. In *C. paleatus*, courtship is brief, with the male swimming over the female. Finally, with the male underneath, they take up a crossed position and the female swims up with four eggs clasped in her ventral fins. These she deposits on a leaf, and the process is repeated. It is not yet clear where the eggs are fertilized. Some observers allege that the female takes sperm into her mouth and sprays it over the eggs, but others deny this. Of *C. aeneus*, it is also said that the male spreads sperm on the glass, and that the female follows and lays her eggs. In *Corydoras* the best stimulus to spawning is said to be a gradual overnight cooling from 30 °C down to 18 °C or even 15 °C. Generally speaking the catfishes are a problem bunch when it comes to breeding, and we clearly have much to learn about them.

Loaches of various species have also been known to breed in the aquarium, but rarely to order. *Acanthophthalmus kuhlii* (coolie loach) and some related species have been bred through the use of hormone injections.

Some of the nandids are easy to breed. *Badis badis* spawns rather like the cichlids and guards the young for a time, and so do *Polycentrus schomburgkii* and *Monocirrhus polyacanthus* (leaf fishes). *Polycentropsis abbreviata*, on the other hand, builds a bubblenest. The male guards the young as in the anabantids. Other nest-builders include the sunfishes (Centrarchidae). The male of *Elassoma evergladei* (pygmy sunfish) builds a nest at the bottom of the tank and guards the eggs, as does the male of various sticklebacks (Gasterosteidae). The male bumblebee goby (*Brachygobius*) also guards the young but does not build a nest.

For all these fishes it is merely necessary to have them in a tank together, except perhaps the *Corydoras*, with which orthodox spawning techniques may be used. Naturally, if you wish to breed them, you will provide plenty of shelter, place only the desired species in the tank, and feed them plenty of live food.

The chocolate gourami (*Sphaerichthys osphromenoides*) is a mouthbrooder. It spawns rather like the dwarf gourami and the male then takes the fertilized eggs into his mouth. Some 12-14 days later the male spits out 20-50 young. Spawning and successful culture have taken place at high temperatures, around 30 °C, and at a pH of 5.0 to 5.6.

The medaka or rice fish (*Oryzias latipes*) provides the final variation that we shall mention, in that although pairing takes place as usual in the egg scatterers, the eggs stick to the female's vent in a cluster, later to be brushed off at random onto plants. This is one of the few fishes which, although it does not take care of its young, also does not eat them. The White Cloud Mountain minnow (*Tanichthys albonubes*) is also fairly safe with its parents.

# CHAPTER TWELVE

## Feeding and Rearing the Fry

Two fish foods have revolutionized the rearing of fry. These are microworms and brine shrimp. Before they were available or had been popularized, raising a tank of two or three hundred young fishes was quite a task, particularly if the fry were very small at first and required an extensive period of small live food. Commercially made suspensions of nutrients now available have made it convenient to feed newly hatched fishes without live food as a start, but it is rare to hear of outstanding successes with them. Such preparations can be kept floating in the tank by mild aeration and will be taken by the young of many species. Older techniques were to shake up egg yolk, powdered dry food or yeast and feed similarly, or to prepare infusorial cultures, which are indeed still needed with very small fry.

Not all fry can be started on microworms or brine shrimp, and some have to be supplied with smaller food for a few days, but a surprising number can eat them from the start, especially the young of the microworm, though the parents may be too big. Thus, newly hatched giant danios (*Danio aequipinnatus*), zebra danios (*Brachydanio rerio*), glowlight tetras (*Hemigrammus erythrozonus*), head and tail light tetras (*Hemigrammus ocellifer*) and most of the barbs, to cite only a few examples, can take brine shrimp as soon as they are free-swimming. It is not the size of the young that counts as much as their mouth capacity or even their willingness to accept a particular food. With any given species, it is easy to see whether they are eating brine shrimp because their bellies show a red color even when only one or two have been eaten. It may be observed that not all the fry are taking them, perhaps only the largest, and it must then be decided whether to arrange for supplementary feeding of the unlucky ones or to let them starve and raise only the biggest starters. It may be added that either of these live foods appears to be a complete and satisfactory food on its own. There is no need to worry about varying the fishes' diets in the early stages if these foods are given.

In what follows, therefore, it is to be understood that, if one or both of these foods are available (and they are easy to get), they will normally be used as soon as possible. Discussion of alternative feeding methods is included because these are sometimes needed before the fry can take bigger food and may be needed as emergency substitutes at any time.

## FOOD AND FOOD SIZES

*Grade 1*, the smallest foods, includes one-celled algae, bakers' yeast, some infusoria, infusions of hard-boiled egg yolk thoroughly shaken in water, or *very* finely ground dry shrimp or other dry food. Some particles of dry food will always be too big, but many can be taken by even the smallest fry. The finer commercial liquid suspensions also fall in Grade 1.

The unicellular algae are supplied as green water, which will also contain infusoria. Fry such as those of the dwarf gourami (*Colisa lalia*) and the Siamese fighting fish (*Betta splendens*) need a start with green water for just a day or two. Naturally, it is best to spawn the parents in green water if this is possible, but such a maneuver is sometimes undesirable because of possible difficulties in catching the female.

Yeast must be used with discretion, just a drop or two of a thick suspension being enough, and it has the advantage of being a live food. An egg suspension is prepared by shaking a small nugget of hard-boiled egg yolk in a bottle with 50 to 100 ml of water until a cloudy suspension results. There are some excellent preparations now on the market which may be used for very small fry instead of egg or yeast suspensions. Those already made up in tubes merely have to be dropped into the tank as needed. Very fine dry food is best prepared in a pepper mill or by grinding it between smooth, flat surfaces for a considerable time. Fry will often only take moving food; therefore a very gentle aeration current helps; use not enough to exhaust the fry but sufficient to keep the food gently moving.

*Grade 2*, the next size of food, is often small enough for starting. These foods are microworms, newly hatched brine shrimp, larger infusoria, small rotifers, finely shredded earthworms, or finely ground dry food. Again, gentle aeration helps with the inert foods and with microworms, which do not always swim up into the water very much. When brine shrimp are given, a light placed directly over the tank attracts the shrimp upwards and keeps them swimming in the water. Otherwise, they may collect at the bottom of the tank, remain uneaten, die, and foul the tank.

When Grade 2 dry or shredded food is used, the time has come to introduce small snails to consume unwanted residues.

*Grade 3* is suitable for all fry after a few weeks and for large newly hatched fry or newly born live-bearer young. It consists of small sifted *Daphnia*, "Grindal" worms, *Cyclops*, newly hatched mosquito larvae, large rotifers, chopped white worms and small granule dry food. Although foods of Grade 2 are still quite suitable for older fry or large newly hatched fry, they *can* take Grade 3.

*Grade 4* is suitable for half-grown fry (2 to 3 cm long). These may be given *Daphnia*, mosquito wrigglers, small chopped earthworms, young unwanted fry of other species, and medium sizes of dry food. Even these fishes may be fed on microworms or newly hatched brine shrimp, on which they thrive as long as they are given enough of it. Brine shrimp may with advantage be grown larger for a few days by feeding them a little yeast, and in the process they will increase severalfold in food value per pinch of eggs originally hatched. For the first two days or so, however, they merely consume the contents of their own yolk sac.

## INFUSORIAL FEEDING METHODS

The need for a continuous supply of live food or of moving suspended food particles in the early days of the life of the fry may be supplied by drip feeding. Many successful breeders never use this method, and it is certainly not necessary, but perhaps an equal number feel happier if they do supply it. Since one purpose of keeping fishes is to enjoy feeding and caring for them as well as looking at them, why not do it if you like to?

When a spawning is planned, an infusorial culture should be on the way if it is likely to be needed. But if it is not produced, use an egg or yeast suspension instead. To feed by drip, it is necessary to siphon the culture very slowly over into the tank. It is not usually necessary to supply a drain for overflow, but a gadget for the purpose will also be described.

The main difficulty in drip feeding is usually to get a slow enough drip. A 1.5 mm (internal diameter) glass tube is bent into a broad square "U" with one leg bent into a smaller "U" and then one of its legs into an even smaller "U." The long leg of the large "U" is inserted into a cork or other float. This diameter tubing fills itself by capillary action and will drip at one drop per minute (3 ml per hour) or faster, as long as the double "U" end of the tubing is bent upwards. If it faces downwards, the minimum speed will be about 40 drops per mintue, and that is too fast for most cultures. The rate is controlled by raising or lowering the tube in the float. Very slow drip rates are best prevented from stopping because of surface tension effects by slipping a piece of tubular tape, wick, or shoelace over the dripping end. A 1.5 mm siphon is self-starting and can be used in the tank as an overflow drip of similar design.

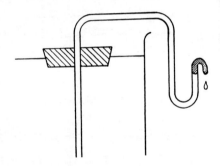

A controllable slow drip feed.

An alternative drip feed is a wick or piece of cloth, but this may filter off too much of the culture, leaving behind a rich medium and delivering a very thin one. Actively feeding fry will eat continuously at the rate of several small infusoria per minute; therefore, a tank of, say, 200 fry needs some 60,000 organisms per hour. A rich culture may supply 100 to 200 very small organisms per drop; hence a drip rate of about 300 per hour or five per minute might be right, but only experience and rough counting of both culture and fry numbers can tell. Fry feeding on pure *Paramecium* cultures need fewer of this larger infusorian.

The number of infusoria needed per day can be dumped into the tank in two or more doses and will not overpopulate the tank while being eaten, as long as the fry are not extremely crowded. That is why drip feeding is rarely a must, but the dumping has to be done with reasonable foresight and careful checks on the condition of the tank. Watch the fry, see that they are eating, and estimate, even if only roughly, the proper amount of culture to feed. Quite wide margins are tolerated and only normal care has to be taken, but *some* care is essential. Remember that not very much is needed at the start, but the rate at which the fry require food is always increasing as they grow and larger amounts must be supplied.

From the start, therefore, it is perfectly feasible to raise fry with two feeds per day, morning and evening (but give them light to feed by). Occasionally a spawning may be lost because of a foul tank or unnoticed underfeeding, but the numbers of spawnings that can be coped with by this simple scheme more than make up for this mishap. Anyway, spawnings are lost more frequently by older methods. There are certain advantages, too, in the infrequent feeding technique. For example, when a mass of food is given all at once, the greediest fishes cannot eat it all and must temporarily leave some for the weaker ones. This means that the weaker ones get some food, whereas with drip feeding they may starve if the stronger and greedier fry sit under the drip and grab it all. This does happen, and it is probably another reason why drip feeding is not always very successful.

## LATER FEEDING

If an infusorial, green water, or other fine-food start has been necessary, try after a couple of days to substitute a Grade 2 food. Give them some and with a hand lens watch what happens. See if the food is taken, and try to estimate if *all* the fry are taking it. If not, give both foods together for a day or two, and so make the change-over gradually. Do exactly the same when attempting to change from any food to another food of larger size, and do not starve your smaller fishes. They will not turn out to be runts unless you force them to.

By this method, most if not all of the fry can be brought along as a nice even batch. The exception is goldfish, among which a spawning may be so variable that all sorts of fry sizes and quality are encountered despite the most careful feeding. But with tropicals, which breed true, 10% of runts is as much as should be expected. The rest will vary in size a bit but should not show the enormous variation so often seen in which the largest fry finally eat the smallest and so even things up a bit. This is due to inadequate or inappropriate feeding, or both, and can be avoided.

As the fry grow, even if they have been raised entirely on live food for the first few weeks, it is quite in order to start substituting a proportion of dry food. Keep to live food all the time if you can, but do not starve the fishes by trying to economize in a 100% live-food campaign. As with full-grown fishes, fry after the first few weeks do well on about 50% live food and quite well on only 25% or 30% if really necessary.

Although goldfish fry can tolerate lower temperatures, they do better if kept at 21° to 24°C during the early growing period but do not thrive so well much above 24°C. Their feed can be the same as outlined above.

## SPACE REQUIREMENTS AND CULLING

Young fry can stand much crowding. Even when 1 cm in length, most species can be packed some nine or ten to the liter. An outstanding exception is the goldfish, in which fry need good space after the first few weeks for adequate growth and must be sorted out fairly early. As long as aeration is supplied the fry of nearly all tropicals can be kept in the small 10- to 20-liter breeding tank advocated for the first six weeks unless there is a spawning, say, of over 250 per tank. In such a case they will do better if given more room after the first four weeks. Goldfish fry will stand equal crowding at first, but after two to three weeks they should be much more liberally provided with space, so that by the time they are six to eight weeks old there should be only about one or two per liter, and progressively fewer as they grow up.

In the goldfish, this process will be accompanied in the usual course of events by quite severe culling, so that the capacity of the aquarium is not so badly strained as it might seem at first sight. Culling can start as soon as you can see body and finnage shapes and sizes. Culling for color is impossible until much later. With all types of goldfish, good shape, finnage, and color are attained by only a very small number—less than 1% is usual. With the fancy types, vast numbers of "throwbacks" occur, some of which are worth keeping as good examples of different classes, but many are useless. The genetics of goldfish are complex, no doubt made so in part by the reluctance of breeders to inbreed consistently and so help to clean stocks up.

Thus, with the goldfish, culling can be severe. It all depends on your standards and on how many relatively inferior fish you wish to keep for disposal or pond stocking. Few will be worth keeping for further breeding. With tropicals, which throw far fewer abnormal or undesirable forms, it is usually the aim to keep most of the spawning, rejecting only a few runts or badly shaped individuals during the first weeks, and later selecting those which grow best and have the nicest general appearance for breeding. There are few standards for tropicals as compared with goldfish, and it is much more of a personal affair as to which type of fish you like best for breeding, the full-bodied or the slimmer fish, the giant or the smaller sized, perhaps more brilliant adult. Variation is in any case much less.

When a batch of tropicals has reached a size at which they can be safely moved from the premises, which occurs after six to ten weeks, depending on their diet, numbers, growing space provided, and temperature at which they have been kept, a number may be kept for future breeding. These, of which at least a dozen should be selected, will be given the best of food and conditions and may be ready for breeding within another few weeks, or perhaps not for a year, according to species. It is usual to select the best of the largest fishes, if there is much size difference, for it is a curious trait of fish fanciers that they confine their attentions to small species that are easy to handle and are not too bulky for life in home aquaria and then do their best to grow them as large as possible. This cannot happen with goldfish, since the biggest ones and the fastest growers are the throwbacks. Big fish are not necessarily the healthiest, although they are unlikely to be unhealthy, nor are they necessarily of the best shape or color. Yet, selection for size is likely to be of more influence than any other single factor, and its effect must be kept in careful check by the thoughtful breeder. Do not pick runts, but do not just pick the whoppers, even if they look good. Medium-sized fishes may be just as healthy or even the healthiest, resembling ourselves in that regard. Think of the effect on the human race if no one under 180 cm were allowed to breed and no attention were paid to other desirable characters.

## RIDDING OF PESTS

If the brood tank has been adequately disinfected, pests will have been eradicated at the start. However, they may get in or be introduced during rearing, but they will usually be at a disadvantage compared with the fry, which will often eat them. Young snails at the fry-raising stage are a help, not a pest, and should be encouraged. The same is true of planaria and many other organisms which were unwanted earlier. However, a few undesirables are liable to crop up, the worst of which is *Hydra*. *Hydra* feeds on small organisms and is very likely to appear in swarms when these abound, as in the brood tank. If present early, it is a menace to small fry; later it may compete with them for food.

In nearly all cases *Hydra* may be eliminated in the presence of fry by adding ammonium nitrite or sulphate to the water. The appropriate quantity is 100 mg per liter, added already dissolved in a little water, and well stirred up. This is surprising in the light of the nitrogen cycle and the toxicity of ammonia and nitrites but it works, and the fry must be remarkably resistant at that stage. The temperature is then raised by 3° to 6°C if possible. It is essential not to allow the ammonium salt solution to form a layer at the bottom, which will kill the fry. The treatment is best given after feeding the *Hydra* well. They do not disappear dramatically but fade away over the course of the next few days. A second treatment may be given if necessary, but if, for some reason, that is no good, further treatments should not be applied.

Blue-green algal or bacterial film sometimes settles on the surface of newly set up aquaria and on breeding tanks also. A piece of newspaper drawn across the surface is about the best cleaning agent in this and similar conditions. The scum adheres to the paper and is mostly removed. Addition of healthy filamentous green algae to the tank often holds other types and even bacteria in check, and it is a fine environment for young fry, as it is a very good oxygenator and provides food in the form of the spores and the microorganisms it harbors.

# CHAPTER THIRTEEN

## Diseases and Parasites

The treatment of diseases in fishes, as in humans, depends on diagnosis and knowledge of which drugs may effect a cure. For the amateur, correct diagnosis is often very difficult and it is too often the same for the professional. However, some of the commonest diseases have naturally been most investigated and methods of treatment have been developed. The obvious and most easily treated conditions are external parasitism and infection, or disease due to poor aquarium conditions. Internal parasites or infections often do too much damage before being recognized, and treatment may be ineffective; it is in any case more difficult.

Dealing with fish diseases in freshwater aquaria demands attention to factors other than just treating the fish. An effective drug for this purpose may kill plants or stain everything in the tank, yet it may be undesirable to remove the fishes for separate treatment—difficulty of capture, the disease still present in the tank, no facilities for quarantine, are examples of complicating factors. Hence a preferred cure (if it exists) should not harm plants or other tank inhabitants, not color or cloud the water unduly, not stain plastic or other equipment. For this reason, the use of potassium permanganate, methylene blue, and some antibiotics will not usually be advocated even though they are effective against certain diseases.

There are many preparations on the market for the cure of fish diseases, some containing the same drugs as are recommended here; others are mixtures of several drugs. When the contents are specified, you can check whether any particular remedy provides the same treatment as given below; if so it may be used instead of going to the trouble of making up your own. Otherwise, it is unwise to use an unknown preparation. Regrettably some of those available are not effective, while others employ chemicals which stain the tank contents and kill plants—some even stain the fishes!

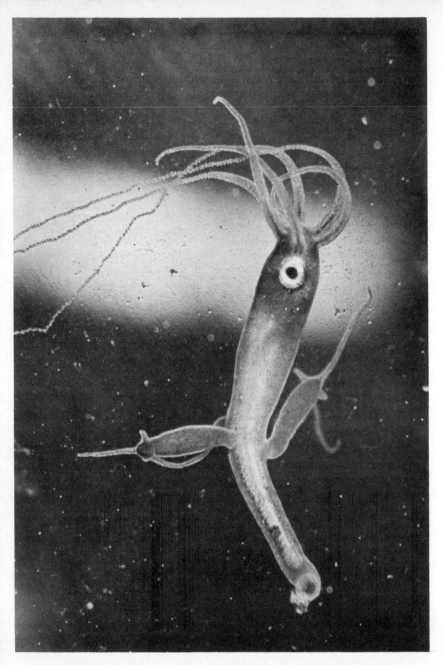

This photo of a *Hydra* that has just eaten a fish fry, visible through its translucent body wall, emphasizes the danger of having a predatory animal in your fish tank.

230

The tail region of a goldfish with a heavy infection of the common aquarium fish disease "ich."

A photomicrograph of a fin section of a fish with encysted cells of *Ichthyophthirius multifiliis.* Disease organisms are usually treated with certain dyes for greater visibility and specific diagnosis.

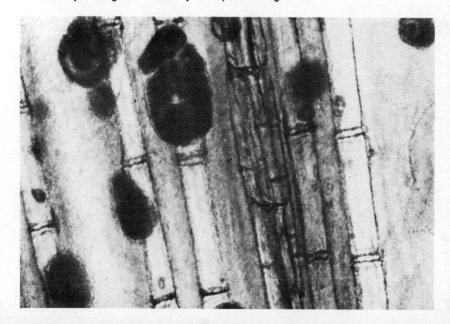

It is possible to treat an aquarium in a prophylactic manner so that the commonest diseases will be eliminated from the start, and this is now becoming popular in marine aquaria because of the frequency of an outbreak in a newly set-up tank if it is not done. However, the freshwater aquarist, although his new tank is liable to the new-tank syndrome already mentioned, is less frequently plagued with such problems. Care in selecting your dealer, in selecting fishes even from him, and in your own handling of them will usually be a sufficient safeguard. The following pages are for when it isn't! Only some of the commoner and more serious diseases are described below, and specialist books should be consulted for descriptions and suggested treatments of others.

## WHITE SPOT OR ICH

This disease, often called "ich" (pronounced *ick*) because of the systematic name of the parasite, is caused by a protozoan, a one-celled animal called *Ichthyophthirius multifiliis*. This has a free-swimming stage that infects the fishes, and it is in this stage that it can most readily be killed by drugs. In this stage, it is very small, about 0.35 mm in diameter, and moves through the water by means of little hairs, or *cilia*, which row it around by regular beating movements. Because of the filtering effect of the gills and the mass of water passing through them, many of the parasites will be trapped there and become embedded, thence developing into relatively large white nodules up to 1.0 mm in size. A few of the free-swimming parasites will also come up against the fins or body, and so at the beginning of an attack of white spot only a few spots will be seen, most on the fins or tail. The rate at which more become obvious depends on many conditions, but by the time the fishes are heavily infested on fins and body, they will usually be very sick, because their gills will be even more heavily laden with the parasites and breathing will be difficult.

In the fish, the parasite penetrates the mucus and outer skin layers (outer epidermis) and becomes covered by an epidermal layer giving rise to a small cyst. This irritates the fish, and as the parasite grows it feeds on red blood cells and skin cells. After a few days it is fully grown, bores its way out of the skin, and falls to the bottom of the tank or onto plants or rocks. It then forms a cyst of its own, inside which rapid cell division results in an average of about 1000 young which swim up into the water seeking a host. The whole cycle takes about four weeks at 10°C but is reduced to about five days at 27°C.

If they do not find a host, the young parasites die within two to three days, but unfortunately there appear to be stages in which the adult may remain incompletely developed in the skin of a lightly infected fish and so remain a menace in an apparently healthy fish. Thus, the tank may be sterilized as far as ich is concerned by removing all fishes and waiting a few days, but complete eradication from the fishes themselves is difficult.

*Symptoms* of the disease should by this time be apparent. The fishes show irritation and glance off rocks and plants; gill irritation causes them to rub the nose and head region, although this does not help them. The white spots may be visible, but must be searched out in the early stages as an aid to diagnosis. Fins and tail become clamped as the disease progresses, and eventually masses of spots, which may coalesce, become visible in untreated fishes.

*Treatment* must be external and must be aimed at the free-swimming stage. Hence raising the temperature in tropical tanks hastens development and aids a rapid cure by drugs, but there is a limit to this in coldwater tanks. With certain tropical species such as anabantoids and many loaches, heat alone may be effective as they can stand temperatures in the range of 32° to 34°C and the parasite cannot (mainly due to its sensitivity to low oxygen content of the water). With most other fishes, chemical treatment is needed in addition. The drug of choice is *quinine hydrochloride* at 30 mg per liter (1 in 30,000). Quinine sulphate, which is less soluble, may be used if the hydrochloride is not available. Dissolve the total dose in a liter or so of water and add it to the tank one third at a time at 12-hour intervals with brisk aeration if possible. At least stir the water well if aeration is not in use. The water may cloud a little, but this will clear, and most plants will not be affected. It will not be necessary to change the water afterwards; just let nature and your periodic partial water changes take care of the residue of the drug.

The cure is not dramatic, as spots on the fish are not much affected. They fall off in the course of the next few days and the fishes should remain clear thereafter, but any sign of reappearance of spots indicates the need for further treatment. Do not give this unless necessary, as it can be hard on both plants and fishes. The dose recommended is aimed at eradication of the disease and is near to the tolerance limit of some plants and some fishes too. An acid pH, down to 6.0, also helps, but make any such adjustment *after* adding the quinine. Do *not* remove fishes from the tank for a month after treatment, or they may infect another tank, and appear particularly liable to do so. Perhaps quinine helps to cause the resting stage mentioned above in the skin of the fish.

Antibiotics can cure white spot but are still a rather costly method of doing it. Their real advantage is that some can effect a cure even on the fish; thus penicillin is said to clear the condition in a few hours at a concentration of only about 500 units per liter. Other reports would seem to be less optimistic, up to 12,500 units per liter being a more usual dose. Wider spectrum antibiotics are also useful, but some cloud the water, cause frothing, and may discolor the water as they break down. On the whole, antibiotic treatment for protozoal diseases would not be expected to meet with great success, and greater cost plus the danger of causing resistant strains to develop point to their avoidance where possible.

## VELVET

This disease, also known as rust disease, is caused by another protozoon (but classified by some authors as an algae species), *Oodinium limneticum* or *O. pullularis* (and perhaps other species), which have a life-history similar to that of white spot. The creature is a dinoflagellate, which means that it swims by flagellae, whip-like processes, although there are only two in this instance, a long and a short one. Smaller than the free-swimming *Ichthyophthirius*, at only about 0.01 mm in diameter, it also settles down on the fish, adhering at first by its longer flagellum, later putting out pseudopodia, or finger-like processes which invade the skin and give it a firmer grip. In the earlier stages, it may move a little while still attached to the skin. It feeds on the host, but also contains chlorophyll, the green pigment which enables plants to build up organic substances from gases in the

234

air, and in *Oodinium* it performs a similar function and helps to give the "rusty" appearance. Encystment occurs on the fish, but in contrast to white spot, the free-swimming stage is said by some to be produced while the cyst is in the skin, and it does not drop off until about 200 young have been released. Others contradict this and describe a free cyst as with white spot. It doesn't make much difference to the aquarist, except that if fishes were removed from a tank and the first account were true, once the free-swimming parasites had died off the tank should be free of infection. Unfortunately, we don't know how long the free-swimming stage lives, so that it is difficult to test the theory.

*Symptoms:* The appearance of velvet is like a golden or brownish dust over the fins and body, smaller than white spot, and which may show the movement described above. Symptoms of irritation, shortage of oxygen uptake (rapid respiration) and fin clamping also occur, and the gills will usually be the first affected, followed by the general surface of the fish. Due to its small size, the earlier phases of infestation with the parasite may be hard to see, so take care to examine any suspect carefully, from different angles with oblique lighting if possible, and you may be horrified to realize that some of the fishes in a tank carry a heavy infection. The disease affects different species to a surprisingly variable degree; danios are particularly susceptible, but often show little discomfort even when covered with parasites. However, as the disease is highly catching and a killer in the end, particularly of young fishes or fry, it should be eradicated as soon as detected.

*Treatment* is best with copper, at a concentration of approximately 0.02 mg per liter, to be repeated *once* in a few days if necessary. If using the easily available blue crystals of copper sulphate, 0.02 mg per liter of copper is contained in 0.1 mg per liter of crystals, so that a stock solution of copper sulphate crystals should be made in distilled water (not tap water) at a concentration of 0.25% and 1 ml per 5 liters added to the aquarium to be treated. As with white spot, the cure is not immediate, but no new velvet parasites should be able to survive and settle on the fish, those already present gradually disappearing. Heat hastens the process and thus helps towards a quicker cure. Acriflavin (Trypaflavine) or Monacrin may be used instead of copper, at a strength of 0.2% stock solution, adding up to 1 ml per liter. In a suitable situation, the addition of a teaspoonful of salt per 5 liters may be made, which helps the action of the drug. As acriflavine and similar drugs are said to sterilize fishes if left in contact with them for too long, the water should be gradually changed after a cure has been effected.

Copper is not effective against white spot, and acriflavine, etc. are poorly so, while quinine is useless for velvet. It is therefore essential to diagnose correctly which disease is present, if the cures recommended above are to be used. If you cannot be sure which disease is present, or if you suspect that whatever is infecting the fishes is neither disease, although similar to them (there are others), use an antibiotic. Chloromycetin (chloramphenicol) is effective against the whole group and is available in preparations intended for animal use at a cheaper price than medical capsules, etc. It is an antibiotic of choice because it is not much used in human medicine, thus we avoid creating drug-resistant strains, it is colorless and does not harm plants. The water may go transiently cloudy, but should clear up without trouble. The effective dosage is usually between 10 to 20 mg per liter.

## FUNGUS

A group of fungi of the genera *Saprolegnia* and *Achlya,* and no doubt others, attack freshwater, particularly coldwater, fishes. The spores of these fungi are everywhere, floating even in the air. Luckily, fungus attacks only weakened or damaged fishes and so is an individual rather than a group or aquarium-wide problem. If only one or two fishes in a tank are affected, it is much better to net them out and to treat each with a fungicidal bath. Fungus may attack wounds, damage due to white spot or other infestations, or even get a hold on undamaged highly susceptible fishes. Threads of fungus, which eventually form a network below the surface of the skin, spread from a center of infection and eventually produce tufts of external *hyphae* which may be profuse enough to look like cotton wool. These form spore bodies, from which swimming *zoospores* are eventually freed and infect other fishes, but only if they too are weak or damaged. If left untreated, once it has a hold fungus will spread until it kills the fish, damaging tissues as it does so. Other forms of reproduction also occur, as in many plants—fungus is a plant.

*Symptoms* are a gray or whitish growth in the skin of the fish, often associated with visible damage, and may occur anywhere on body or fins. Tufts of external hyphae will eventually give a cotton-wool appearance. The fish is not distressed, at least at first, unless already showing distress from an untreated precursor such as white spot. It may show loss of parts of fins, tail or skin, but not the irritation typical of white spot or velvet.

*Treatment* is with malachite green (zinc-free) or brilliant green in a separate bath for 30 seconds, at a strength of approximately 60 mg per liter. Repeat treatments may be given if necessary. The fungus is stained by the dye and killed; usually it drops off in a few hours. The hyphae below the skin may survive a single treatment, but often seem to be sufficiently affected in any but the heaviest attacks to die off also. It seems to be unwise to treat the whole tank with such dyes at lower concentrations, as poor or even toxic results have been described.

If a lot of the fishes have fungus, a different approach must be used. This employs phenoxethol (2-phenoxyethanol), at 1% in distilled water. Add 10 ml of this solution per liter of aquarium water to be repeated *once only* if necessary. Three treatments within a few days can be toxic. It is necessary to use such large volumes of phenoxethol solution because the drug, an oily liquid, is only sparingly soluble in water. Typically, the fungus disappears within a day, so that repeat treatments should rarely be necessary.

## MOUTH FUNGUS

Very similar in appearance to ordinary fungus, but confined usually to the mouth, this "fungus" is actually caused by a bacterial infection which puts out filaments of a fungus-like appearance. It is a dangerous disease of tropical rather than cold-water fishes and can kill rapidly.

*Symptoms:* The causative organism is *Chondrococcus columnaris*. The infection starts with a white line around the lips and proceeds to outgrowths of chains of bacteria (hence the specific name *columnaris*). The toxins produced by the bacteria and the inability of the fish to eat combine to cause its rapid demise.

237

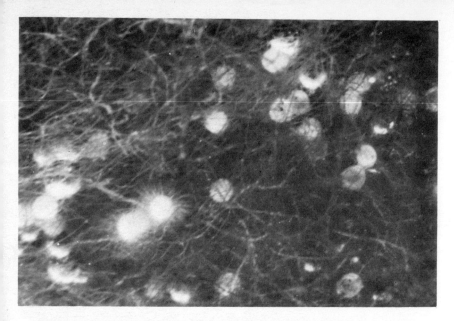

Infertile and dead eggs are very susceptible to fungusing. The infection spreads quickly and will suffocate live eggs within a short time.

One quickly realizes that his paradise fish, *Macropodus opercularis,* is afflicted with pop-eye, but knowing what caused the condition will require some investigation. Many diseases and some environmental conditions can produce pop-eyes.

**Right:** Tail rot or fin rot progresses very slowly and often affects only damaged or weak fishes. Fin damage is a common occurrence in many fishes during courtship. **Below:** The tailless condition of this young cichlid is of genetic origin, not infectious but heritable.

*Treatment* is best given to the whole tank, as the bacteria will be present everywhere and further infection will otherwise occur. Phenoxethol treatment as described above is said to be effective, which if true, relieves the aquarist of deciding whether he is dealing with true fungus or mouth fungus. The author has not tried phenoxethol for mouth fungus, but in common with others finds antibiotics, either penicillin or chloromycetin effective. As the disease is so dangerous, it is felt that this is an instance in which the use of an antibiotic is justified. Penicillin should be given in a single treatment of 10,000 units per liter, a second dose within a day or two being added if necessary. Chloromycetin should be given at 10 to 20 mg per liter also to be repeated if necessary. A cure should result in four or five days, and signs of recovery and lack of further infection should be seen within two days.

## BACTERIAL INFECTIONS IN GENERAL

There is a multitude of mainly externally manifest bacterial infections which attack fishes and for which individual treatments are only sometimes known. Often the fish is infected within as well as on the skin and fins, etc., so that external treatment may be less effective than internal treatment. If the infection appears to be fairly mild, even if widespread, and is not killing the fishes, or at least not more than a small proportion of them, treatment of the whole tank with a disinfectant should be tried first, together with a general clean-up, increased aeration, and light feeding. The diagnosis of these many diseases is empirical, and only in a few cases is the causative organism known.

*Symptoms* of some of the more common infections by which they can be distinguished from those above are clamping of fins and tails with blood streaks or ragged areas, in extreme cases dropping off of pieces of tissue (*tail or fin rot*), blood streaks on the body or ulcerated patches on the body (*red pest*), raising of scales with or without redness (one form of *dropsy*), discoloration of the skin in patches or more extensively (which may also be caused by protozoal diseases and thus need treatment as for white spot), emaciation (*tuberculosis*).

*Treatment*, if applied to the whole tank water, should be with acriflavine, as for velvet, but omitting any addition of salt, or with a wide spectrum antibiotic. Except for special diseases, penicillin is not usually effective against bacteria in the fish tank, because it does not affect Gram-negative organisms responsible for most bacterial diseases. Chloromycetin remains the most useful antibiotic for reasons already given, but some of the newer wide-spectrum derivatives of penicillin (which are quite different from it in action) are also colorless, seemingly non-toxic and effective against many Gram-negative forms and promise to be useful. Ampicillin is one of these but has the unfortunate property of itself irritating the fishes and causing them to scratch on plants and rocks. We must await reports on some of these newer drugs before preferences can be indicated.

In many cases, a better, cheaper and more effective way of administering antibiotics for general bacterial infections is in the food. If the disease is in the blood or internal organs, as will often be the case, this is the sensible method of treatment. Although chloromycetin tastes very bitter to us, it doesn't worry fishes and they will eat dry food with about a 1% mixture of the drug as readily as without it. The author has found that up to 1% is harmless to fishes, if not long continued, and while some will escape into the water, only a very low concentration results which probably has no effect on other organisms and seems unlikely to cause drug resistance. Thus, if 1 gm of food is fed to an average tank of fishes, and this is quite a lot of dry food, it will contain, at 1%, 10 mg of drug. Even if all were to escape into the water, an average tank would be receiving less than 0.25 mg per liter per feed. Antibiotics can be used even with tubifex or chopped frozen or fresh foods, but not of course with other live foods.

For preference, a powdery or granular dry food should be thoroughly mixed with the antibiotic from a medical capsule. This is usually 250 mg per capsule, so that 25 gm of dry food should be used per capsule and fed to the fishes in the usual manner. Keep them somewhat hungry, so that the food does not have time to sink to the bottom and allow the antibiotic to dissolve in the water. Remember that such a technique is of no use for purely external diseases such as white spot or velvet, as it does not get effective amounts of drug to the skin surface and the parasites do not appear to feed on enough host material to absorb a lethal quantity. The free-swimming stages will also remain unaffected.

# ICHTHYOPHONUS

This is a common fungal disease somewhat resembling tuberculosis in its effects but caused by *Ichthyosporidium hoferi* and other similar organisms. It commences internally and is usually acquired from infected food or fish droppings. The parasites invade the bloodstream and may infect any part of the body, but a clear description of the life cycle and the infective phase has not been seen by the author. Ichthyophonus may reproduce locally in the fish, causing cysts in various organs and sometimes on the surface of the body, and symptoms will vary a great deal according to the severity and location of the invasion.

*Symptoms* may include sluggish movements, loss of equilibrium, hollow belly, cysts or sores (often yellow, brown or black) on the surface of the body, and tail or fin rot often caused by secondary infection. The disease is difficult to diagnose because of its great variety, but should always be suspected if an attempted but ineffective cure for another disease has been given. The disease only proceeds rapidly at high temperatures and will remain dormant in coldwater fishes for months.

*Treatment* is very difficult, and if there is only one infected fish it is best killed before (we hope) it has infected others. Two treatments, both in the food, may be tried. Chloromycetin added to the food as described above has been suggested but not positively confirmed as a cure, while a 1% phenoxethol solution added to food (soak the food in it if suitable) has also been advocated. A relative of phenoxethol, *parachlorophenoxethol*, can no longer be recommended, since although it is better than phenoxethol as a cure, it is also very toxic to most species of fish.

# POP-EYE

Exophthalmos, to give pop-eye its more elegant name, may be caused by a variety of conditions, including hormonal imbalance and excessive gas pressure in the blood, often brought about by supersaturation as when water which has been under high mains pressure is placed in the aquarium. It can also be caused by infection, as by ichthyophonus cysts or in cases of dropsy (see below). It is usually confined to a single fish.

*Symptoms* are a protrusion of one or both eyes as in the genetically determined strains of goggle-eyed goldfish. This may subside or progress to the loss of one or both eyes. If in association with an infectious disease, treatment for the disease may cure the condition, but the eye should be examined as carefully as possible to make sure that gas bubbles are not the cause. If they are seen, watch carefully to see if more appear or if they start to coalesce into one or two larger bubbles.

*Treatment* may be impossible, it may be that relevant to the accompanying disease, or specific for gas bubbles, usually nitrogen. Remember that if gas is the cause, this or other fishes may be affected as in human "bends" and show signs of distress or nervous system upset such as odd movements or paralysis. When gas bubbles occur, lower the temperature as far as tolerable to the fishes, to increase gas solubility, decrease any very brisk aeration if feasible, and hope! If one or two very large bubbles are seen in a *badly* affected eye, the rather heroic method of tapping off the gas with a fine hypodermic needle and syringe may be tried. In marine fishes, the excessive use of copper has been reported to cause pop-eye, but no such accounts seem to be available for freshwater fishes. This is worth keeping in mind, however, if copper has recently been used. If so, removal of the copper with activated charcoal or an ion-exchange resin should help.

## DROPSY

This condition is of at least two different types—a general swelling of the body caused by accumulation of fluid in the body cavity, or by a swelling of internal organs such as the liver and intestines. In addition, scale protrusion is often mistaken for true dropsy as it also causes the appearance of body swelling, but with redness of the body surface.

*Symptoms* of true dropsy are bodily or belly swelling, without scale protrusion except in extreme cases, when tremendous body swelling may force it to occur. No external signs of infection are usually seen.

*Treatment* is difficult, as the cause is usually infection by *Aeromonas punctata*, a bacterium affecting internal organs and causing the fluid secretion referred to above. *A. punctata* is usually harmless, but a specially virulent strain causes dropsy, which is usually not highly contagious since the organism only attacks weak fishes. The only reliable treatment appears to be chloromycetin, best fed to the fishes as described for the treatment of bacterial infections in general. As the same treatment is best for scale protrusion, it doesn't really matter which form of the disease is present.

## HOLE-IN-THE-HEAD DISEASE

Pits or depressions in the head region, first a worry in discus fishes, are now found in other species, but mostly the larger fishes.

*Symptoms* are festering sores or holes around the head region, sometimes associated with the lateral line. *Hexamita*, a flagellate, is usually implicated, having entered the body via the gut, travelling presumably in the bloodstream to the head region.

*Treatment* is with the drug metronidazole (Flagyl® ), and is best fed mixed in the food if the fish is eating. If not, you have a problem! However, Dylox® , in a bath, can be effective. This drug is available, with directions, on the market and must be used in a day or two once the vial of powder has been dissolved in the bath. A combined treatment with metranidazole given both by mouth and in the tank has been recommended; use a 1% concentration in any food the fish will take, with 12 mg per liter in the aquarium water, to be added every other day for three treatments.

## SWIM-BLADDER DISEASE

Infections or tank conditions may cause a fish to swim irregularly or even float helplessly at the surface, when it is usually bloated.

*Symptoms* are as above, and due to a distended swim-bladder.

*Treatment* is, if possible, gentle massage or a hypodermic needle to withdraw excess gas. Otherwise, lower the temperature to raise gas solubility and withhold food for a couple of days.

## LARGER PARASITES

So far, microscopic or near microscopic infestations have been considered, but fishes are not infrequently attacked by fish lice and flukes of various kinds. These are often difficult to treat, except by special baths which may demand the removal of the affected fishes from the aquarium, as a short period of "dunking" is required, because the chemicals used would prove toxic or kill plants if left for any length of time in the tank.

*Symptoms* in general are usually of irritation, but often the visible parasite is the most obvious early sign of trouble.

## FISH LICE

The fish louse, *Argulus*, comes in several species and rarely attacks aquarium fishes. However, it may be introduced if fishes are taken from ponds or if *Daphnia* is fed. It is a flattened mite-or spider-like creature about 5 mm long which attaches itself to the skin of its host by means of two large suckers and proceeds to feed on the fish's blood.

*Treatment:* As the louse is large enough to be seen, occasional visitors may be removed by netting the affected fish and plucking the parasite off with a pair of forceps. If there is a heavy infestation or the affected fishes are delicate, it may be best to treat the condition with a bath in 10 mg per liter of potassium permanganate for 10 to 30 minutes. In extreme cases, the whole tank may be treated with the same chemical at 2 mg per liter but the water will have to be siphoned off subsequently, at about half of the total volume per day after the first day until the brown precipitate which forms has been removed.

An alternative treatment is with DFD (difluorodiphenyltrichlormethylmethane) at 1 ml per 10 liters for two to three minutes—the compound is a liquid. Only an external bath at the concentration recommended is feasible—do not introduce the drug into the aquarium.

## ANCHOR WORMS

This parasite, *Lernaea cyprinacea*, is a crustacean, not a worm, but resembles one as it hangs from a deeply embedded "anchor" on the skin of the fish. The female reaches a length of about 2 cm; the male does not attack fishes. The young free-swimming worms penetrate the skin as *nauplii* (an early stage of development), go right into the muscle and develop there for up to several months, eventually emerging and hanging as "worms" into the water. Finally they die, releasing eggs, and the holes they leave behind them are as dangerous as the parasites themselves, as they readily become infected. Fortunately, anchor worms infest mainly large coldwater species such as goldfish and are rarely seen in the tropical tank.

*Treatment* is by DFD bath as decribed above or by touching the visible worms, if only a few are present, with a strong potassium permanganate solution (up to 0.2%), care being taken not to touch the skin more than necessary. It is not possible to remove the worms with forceps. Various suggestions have been made to treat fish lice or anchor worms with insecticides such as gammexane, but until more investigations have been made, the high toxicity of such compounds both to the fishes and in some cases their owners signals caution.

## FLUKES

Much smaller than fish lice or anchor worms, several genera of monogenetic trematodes are a danger in the aquarium. Monogenetic species have only one host and pass from fish to fish, while digenetic species have two hosts, such as a fish and a crustacean, and generations alternate from one host to the other. Some trematodes have three hosts. Clearly, it is the monogenetic varieties that are likely to become dangerous in aquaria, as the two hosts necessary for successful propagation of the others will rarely be present together.

The main genera concerned are *Dactylogyrus, Gyrodactylus* and *Monocoelium*. All are flatworms reaching only 1 mm at maximum and therefore may pass unnoticed in early infestations. They infest skin and gills, much as white spot, and cause the same types of trouble. Differentiation of the species is not necessary for treatment, which is fortunate.

*Symptoms* are pale fishes with drooping fins, rapid respiration if the gills are infected, emaciation and irritation, and mainly occur in coldwater fishes. However, tropicals are attacked from

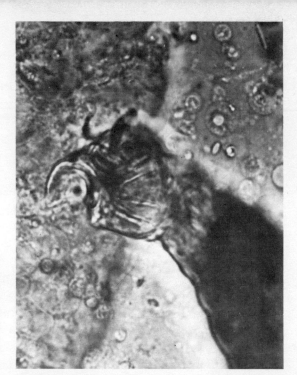

A gill fluke feeding on the gill filament of a fish. A large number of gill flukes is harmful; extensive gill damage leads to loss of gill function and usually ends in death.

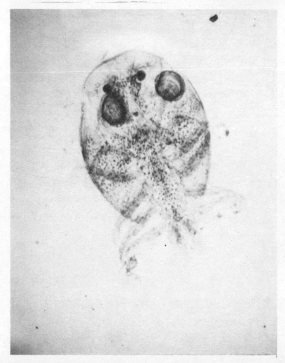

The fish louse *Argulus* is sufficiently large to be visible with the naked eye. Fortunately, this parasite is not commonly found in the home aquarium and if ever present, effective medications are known and available.

time to time and the possibility of a fluke infection should always be remembered when a disease crops up. Look for grayish, minute worms on gills or skin.

*Treatment* is best as for fish lice, with potassium permanganate baths, or if the aquarium is widely infected, with permanganate in the tank, to be removed after treatment. As an alternative, formalin may be used in a bath, but not in the tank. Formalin comes in solution, 40% being common, and a 45-minute bath in 2 ml per 10 liters of water has been recommended.

## NON-INFECTIOUS CONDITIONS

Not all diseases are infectious, or susceptible to treatment if they are. Virus infections cause a number of diseases not listed above, as we have no cure for them. Various tumors, some caused by viruses, some genetic, are not curable, and the sufferer should be painlessly killed, if badly affected. Swordtails are particularly liable to melanotic tumors (dark-colored tumors) which are inherited and untreatable, but these are confined to the darkly pigmented strains.

Various aquarium conditions give rise to symptoms which are sometimes hard to differentiate from infections, so that when no obvious disease can be detected, be ready to suspect:

*Chilling*—a sudden fall in temperature or a chronic exposure to too low a temperature—e.g., a tropical tank kept at 15 °C—may result in *shimmies* without infection, a slow swimming movement without getting anywhere. Raise the temperature to 27° to 30 °C and keep it there for a few days.

*Overheating*—a sudden rise or chronic high temperature—e.g., a tank at 30 °C or higher—may cause distress, gasping at the surface or dashing around the tank. Increase aeration and lower the temperature to normal limits—below 21 °C if possible for a cold tank, below 27 °C but above 21 °C for a tropical tank.

*Poisoning*—patchy discoloration, any oddity of behavior, even blood patches on skin or fins may be due to metallic or other poisoning, such as chlorine (in many raw tap waters), insecticide sprays, tobacco or even an extreme pH. When any such toxicity is suspected, progressive water changes of up to half a tank at a time for water from a pure source or well aged tap water will

Abnormal pigmentation is not contagious and not a threat to tankmates. In some fish species large concentrations of melanin (black pigments) can be possible precursors of cancerous tumors.

usually effect a cure if the condition is not too far advanced. Then look for the source of the trouble—exposed metal, copper piping, the use of too much fresh tap water, an aerator in a room sprayed with fly killer, tobacco under fingernails, pH drop due to pollution or overcrowding and so forth. The metals zinc (galvanizing), copper (new pipes), lead (sinkers), cadmium (electroplating) and nickel are all common sources of trouble and can be highly toxic. Pure lead is safe in freshwater, but not in salt water. The controlled use of copper for velvet disease is one thing; unintended overdosage from a new water supply is another. Some new high-rise buildings have been found to have as high as 80 ppm of copper in the water.

# INDEX

Page numbers printed in italic refer to photographs or illustrations.

canned, 75
frozen, 75
live, 79
manufactured, 74, *107*
natural, 70
other prepared, 79
Forced growth, 194 *et seq.*
Formalin bath, 248
Fountains, 165, 168
Fruit fly, 102
Fry, 103
  feeding, 221
  rearing, 221
  temperature tolerance, 59
*Fundulus chrysotus,* 55
Fungus, 236 *et seq.*, 238

"Gallon" rule, 115
*Gambusia affinis,* 55, 186
*Gammarus,* 87
Garden pool, *58*
Gasterosteidae, 220
Giant danio, 20, 204, 221
Gill irritation, 233
Gills, 35, 50
*Glandulocauda inequalis,* 209
Glass, properties of, 179
Glassworms, 83
Glochidia, *17,* 18
Glowlight tetra, 20, 66, 201, 204, 221
*Gnathonemus petersi, 64*
Goldfish, *39, 41,* 202
  spawning, 209
Gonopodium, 21, *63,* 186
Gourami, 25
Gravel, 141
  depth, 142
  other materials in, 142
  removal and replacement, 137
  washing, 142
Green algae, 15, 138, 201
Green water, 98
Grindal worms, 98, 223
Guppy, *17, 29, 68, 109, 120, 183*
*Gymnocorymbus ternetzi,* 20, 57
*Gyrinocheilus aymonieri, 104*
*Gyrodactylus,* 246

Hair grass, 14
*Haplochromis* species, 30
Hard water, 126
Hardness, 129 *et seq.*, 133
Harlequin fish, 20, *206*
Hatchet fish, 55
Hatching of eggs, 211
Head and tail light fish, 21, 204, 221
Heat loss, 156, 178

calculations, 157
Heat shock, 59
Heaters, *12*
  calculating wattages, 157 *et seq.*
  in parallel, 161
  in series, 161
  submersible, 159
  types, 158
Heating, 145, 151, 177
Heating rooms, 177
*Helostoma temmincki, 68,* 71
*Hemichromis bimaculatus,* 24, 55, *60*
*Hemigrammus caudovittatus,* 55, 70
*H. erythrozonus,* 20, 66, 201, 204, 221
*H. ocellifer,* 20, 183, 204, 221
*Heterandria bimaculata,* 186
*H. formosa, 63,* 186
*Hexamita,* 244
Hole-in-the-head disease, 244
Hornwort, 14
*Hyallela,* 87
*Hydra,* 228, *230*
*Hygrophila,* 14, 29, 30, *36*
*Hyphessobrycon flammeus,* 20, 183, *196*
*H. pulchripinnis, 57,* 202
*H. rosaceus,* 21, 201
*H. serpae,* 21
*Hypostomus plecostomus,* 28

Ich (white spot disease), 232 *et seq.*
Ichthyophonus, 242
*Ichthyophthirius multifiliis, 231,* 232
*Ichthyosporidium hoferi,* 242
Incubation of eggs, 210
Infertile eggs, 210
Infusoria, 70, 99, 222
  culture, 99
  drip feed, 223
Insect larvae, 82
Isolation tank, 183

Jack Dempsey, 24
Japanese live-bearing snail, 15
Jewel fish, 24, 55, *60*
*Jordanella floridae, 60*

Killie fishes, 20, 66, 204 *et seq.*
Kissing gourami, *68,* 71
Kribensis, 77

*Labeotropheus fuelleborni, 195*
Labyrinth, 25, 38
Lateral line, 43, *44*
*Lamprologus brichardi, 53*
Leaf fishes, 220
*Lemna,* 14
Lemon tetra, *56,* 202